T000162b

CULTURE SMART!

ECUADOR

THE ESSENTIAL GUIDE TO CUSTOMS & CULTURE

RUSSELL MADDICKS

KUPERARD

"The real voyage of discovery consists not in seeking new landscapes, but in having new eyes."

Adapted from Marcel Proust, *Remembrance of Things Past.*

ISBN 978 1 78702 300 0

British Library Cataloguing in Publication Data
A CIP catalogue entry for this book is available
from the British Library

First published in Great Britain
by Kuperard, an imprint of Bravo Ltd
59 Hutton Grove, London N12 8DS
Tel: +44 (0) 20 8446 2440
www.culturesmart.co.uk
Inquiries: publicity@kuperard.co.uk

Design Bobby Birchall
Printed in Turkey

ABOUT THE AUTHOR

RUSSELL MADDICKS is a BBC-trained writer, translator, and journalist. A graduate in Economic and Social History from the University of Hull, England, he has spent the last twenty-five years traveling, living, and working in Central and South America, and worked as a Latin American Regional Specialist for BBC Monitoring. A fluent Spanish speaker, he has made many extended trips to Ecuador, one of his favorite South American destinations, where he has explored the length and breadth of the country both for work and for pleasure. He is also the author of *Culture Smart!* guides to Cuba, Mexico, Nicaragua, and Venezuela and the *Bradt Guide to Venezuela*.

CONTENTS

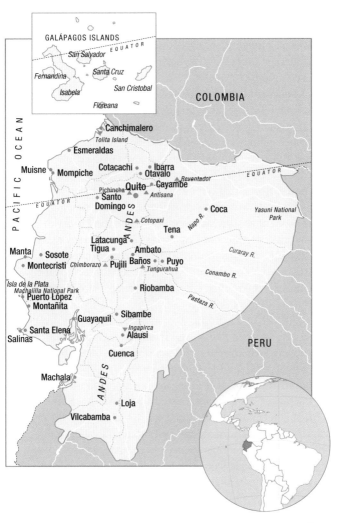

Ecuador may be the fourth-smallest country in South America, but this compact Andean nation punches above its weight in terms of diversity, with a geographical landscape so varied it has been called a microcosm of every micro-climate found in South America.

Squeezed between Colombia and Peru, Ecuador is named for its location on the Equator. It has some of the highest and most active volcanoes in the world; steamy Amazon jungles in the east; a Pacific coast dotted with beach resorts; and, out to sea, the jewel in the country's crown—the fabled Galápagos Islands. Named after giant tortoises that can live for more than 150 years, the Galápagos is where a young Charles Darwin first had the seed of an idea that germinated into the Theory of Natural Selection and Evolution. All this diversity makes Ecuador a magnet for tourists, birdwatchers, mountain trekkers, volunteers, and US retirees looking for a warm, culturally interesting, affordable, and safe place to spend their retirement dollars.

A food lover's dream, the country's cuisine is as diverse as its geography, with village markets offering traditional country-style comfort food, seafood stalls on the beaches of the Pacific serving up delicious ceviches, and gourmet restaurants delivering exquisite fine dining in the cities of Quito, Cuenca, and Guayaquil. Scientists have now firmly established that Ecuador—not Mexico—is the true birthplace of chocolate and that cacao cultivation first began 5,000 years ago in the Amazonian area of Zamora-Chinchipe. So it is no surprise that its premium Arriba cocoa beans are highly coveted by the world's chocolate makers.

Ecuadorians are proud, friendly, hospitable, and hardworking. The country's diverse population reflects a unique blend of cultures, from the traditionally dressed villagers of the Sierra mountains, to the tribal peoples of the Amazonian rainforest, and Afro–Ecuadorians in Esmeraldas and the Chota Valley. To understand the culture in any depth, however, you need to know the complex historical divisions between the highlands and the coast, and the rigid class and racial hierarchy that has dominated the country's history.

In recent years, the far-reaching economic and social progress won under former President Rafael Correa has faltered, while the effects of the coronavirus pandemic exacerbated an economic downturn by halting one of the country's leading sources of income—tourism. There is optimism for the future, however; travelers are returning to Ecuador once more and there is a feeling of anticipation as the country finds its footing under new political leadership.

This updated edition of *Culture Smart! Ecuador* takes you to the heart of this diverse nation to give you an insider's view of the people, their history, and their way of life. It describes the customs and traditions that people hold dear and the attitudes that you are most likely to encounter. Once the ice has been broken, Ecuadorians are fun-loving and extremely sociable. Any effort made to get to know them will be welcomed and reciprocated many times over.

Official Name	República de Ecuador	Pop. 18 million
Capital City	Quito	Pop. 2 million. Altitude 9,350 ft (2,850 m)
Other Major Cities	Guayaquil (pop. 2.6m); Cuenca (330,000); Santo Domingo (322,000)	
Area	99,706 sq. miles (258,238 sq. km)	Fourth-smallest country in South America
Geography	Borders Colombia in the north, Peru in the south and east, and Pacific coast on the west. Straddles the Equator in northwest and includes part of Amazon basin	
Terrain	Diverse. Mountains, snow-covered volcanoes, cloud forests; tropical rainforests, major river systems, coastal lowlands, beaches, islands	
Climate	Coast dry and hot with rainy season downpours; rain forest hot, wet, humid; mountains cool, temperate	Quito temperatures spring-like year-round. Average high of 67°F (19.5°C) and low of 48.5°F (9°C)
Seasons	Dry and rainy seasons vary with altitude. Dry months Sep.–Nov. on coast; Jun.–Oct. in highlands; Nov.–Mar. in the Amazon	Sunrise (± 6:00 a.m.) and sunset (± 6:00 p.m.) throughout the year.

Life Expectancy	Men 74; women 79	
Ethnic makeup	71.9% Mestizo (mixed race); 7.4% Montubio; 7.2% Afro–Ecuadorian; 7% Indigenous; 6.1% White	
Languages	Official language: Spanish 92.83%. 12 indigenous languages	Quechua and Shuar recognized as Official Languages of Intercultural Relations in 2008 Constitution.
Religion	76% Roman Catholic; 15% Protestant/ Evangelical; 1.5% Jehovah's Witness; 7% indigenous beliefs/other	Protestants have made significant gains in recent years.
Government	Democratic Republic with a Unicameral National Assembly elected every four years. President is chief of state and head of government, elected every four years.	Country divided into 24 provinces, each with an administrative capital
Media	Privately owned national newspapers: *El Comercio, El Universal, Hoy*	
Currency	US dollar (US$), divided into 100 cents	GDP per capita US $5,600
Electricity	110 volts, 60 Hz	European appliances need adaptors.
Telephone	International dialing code 593	City codes: Quito 2; Guayaquil 4; Galápagos 5; Cuenca 7
Time Zone	UTC/GMT −5 hours	

CHAPTER ONE

LAND & PEOPLE

Occupying an area of 109,483 square miles (283,561 sq. km), Ecuador is the smallest of the Andean countries and the fourth-smallest country in South America, occupying an area similar to the US state of Colorado.

Straddling the Equator on South America's western coast, Ecuador is bordered to the north by Colombia and to the east and south by Peru. Its long Pacific coastline on the west stretches some 1,452 miles (2,337 km), from the border with Colombia to the border with Peru. Off the coast lie the Islas Galápagos, an archipelago of volcanic islands known for their biodiversity and large number of endemic species.

Due to its position on the Equator, Ecuador has a tropical climate that varies widely over its diverse geographic terrain, encompassing a number of microclimates including Andean mountains; active and inactive volcanoes; montane valleys known as *paramos*; cloud forests; vast stretches of steamy Amazon jungle; a long Pacific coast; and arid deserts. There are four main geographic regions: the Sierra, or Andean highlands,

The Andean peaks of the Yanacocha Reserve.

running from north to south in the center of the country; the Costa, or Pacific coast in the west; the Oriente, or Amazon region, in the east; and the Galápagos Islands.

La Sierra—Andean Mountains and Valleys

Popular with hikers, climbers, and lovers of dramatic mountain landscapes, Ecuador's Andean region covers about 24 percent of the country and offers snow-capped volcanoes and verdant valleys with spring-like temperatures year-round.

The Ecuadorian Andes run from north to south along two mountain chains known as the Eastern Cordillera and the Western Cordillera. Between them is a high intermontane valley that the nineteenth-century Prussian naturalist Alexander von Humboldt dubbed the Avenue of the Volcanoes.

The highest peaks are the volcanoes Chimborazo, at 20,702 feet (6,310 m), Cotopaxi, at 19,347 feet (5,897 m), and Cayambe, at 18,996 feet (5,790 m). Ecuadorians are proud to point out that, due to the bulge at the equator, Chimborazo is the farthest point on the planet from the center of the earth, making it technically higher than Mount Everest. One of the most active volcanoes is Tungurahua at 16,456 feet (5,016 m), which rises above the popular tourist town of Baños, named for its sulfurous hot springs, which are believed to have health-giving properties.

The capital, Quito, is in a mountain valley at 9,350 feet (2,850 m) above sea level, which can give new arrivals prone to altitude sickness slight breathlessness, dizzy spells, and headaches until they acclimatize. Overlooking Quito are the twin peaks of Guagua Pichincha, at 15,696 feet (4,784 m) and Rucu Pichincha, at 15,413 feet (4,698 m).

A view of Quito's Old Town, a UNESCO World Heritage Site.

La Costa—the Pacific Coast

Covering some 25 percent of the country, La Costa comprises a wide coastal belt that runs from the border of Colombia to the border of Peru, and from the sea to the foothills of the Andes. In the north, areas of tropical rainforest are maintained by the high rainfall associated with the warm waters of the El Niño current that sweeps up from Panama. Farther south, cattle ranching and the agricultural production of bananas has seen 98 percent of the native forest cut down. What remains of the rainforest, cloud forest, and dry forest in the mountains along the coastal strip is part of the endangered Tumbes-Chocó-Magdalena biodiversity hotspot, which provides microclimates for hundreds of endemic bird species, rare howler and spider monkeys, and other mammals. Private

The beaches of the Machalilla National Park on the Pacfic coast.

reserves aim to preserve these last remaining areas of native forest. In the south, scrub and deserts predominate on the southern coast due to the drying effects of the Humboldt Current, which brings cold, nutrient-rich water from southern Chile up to the Equator. Although it provides abundant stocks of sardines, anchovies, and mackerel, the Humboldt Current is prone to periodic depletion of fish stocks caused by the El Niño phenomenon.

Guayaquil is the dominant city on the coast and the country's largest port. All along the coast there are beach resorts catering to locals and foreign tourists.

El Oriente—the Amazonian Rainforest

The east of Ecuador is known as El Oriente, a swathe of hot and humid rainforest that covers some 49 percent of the country and teems with tropical wildlife and birds. It is also home to indigenous people, such as the Quechua-speaking Kichwa, and the remote Waorani who, despite the encroachment of loggers and oil companies, live very much as they did before the arrival of Europeans.

Running through this heavily forested region are major rivers, such as the mighty Napo, which starts as meltwater on the glaciers of volcanoes like Cotopaxi, Antisana, and Sichulawa, and is fed by the Coca River before joining the Amazon in Peru. In the lower Oriente around Puyo, the Pastaza River feeds into the Marañón River in Peru. Oriente is home to Ecuador's most important nature parks, such as the Yasuni National Park, a designated UNESCO Biosphere Reserve that has been hailed by ecologists as the most biologically diverse spot on the planet.

Pastaza Valley in the Llanganates National Park, El Oriente.

The region is also the location of the country's principal oil reserves. Past oil drilling that led to the poisoning of rivers and soil with oil spills has shown how environmentally damaging oil extraction can be for these fragile forest environments.

The Galápagos Islands

The eighteen main islands and fifty or so smaller islets of the volcanic Galápagos archipelago are so special, and the wildlife they harbor so distinctive, that they have been described as a showcase of evolution. Located some 600 miles (1,000 km) off the mainland in the Pacific Ocean, the islands were formed from undersea volcanic eruptions from 8 million to 3.5 million years ago and cover an area of 3,090 square miles (8,010 sq. km).

One of three species of land iguana on the Galápagos Islands.

Charles Darwin featured their extraordinary diversity in his book *The Voyage of the Beagle*, which recounts his 1835 visit to the Galápagos, and he later used the example of adaptations among finches on the different islands to support his Theory of Evolution and Natural Selection. In 1978 the Galápagos was the first place on the planet to be declared a UNESCO World Heritage Site.

English pirates used the islands to hide out when targeting Spanish treasure ships, and early maps feature the English names for the islands. They were officially annexed by Ecuador on February 12, 1832.

The main industry is tourism, and, before the coronavirus pandemic, about 170,000 foreign visitors flocked here each year to marvel at the blue-footed boobies, marine iguanas, tame sea lions, and giant tortoises. In the past, there were fears that the growth of tourist infrastructure on the main islands of San Cristobal, Santa Cruz, Floreana, and Isabela, including the growing number of cars, was having an increasingly negative impact on the wildlife and prompted measures aimed at regulating the numbers. Conservationists hope that authorities will employ a more sustainable approach to tourism as the number of visitors rises once again.

PEOPLE

Ecuador's people are as diverse as the country's geography. According to recent figures, approximately 70 percent of the population identify as Mestizos (mixed race), a legacy of the Spanish conquest. Only around 6 percent class themselves as Blancos (white), though they make up the majority of the rich elite in business, land ownership, and politics. They generally claim Spanish descent, although later European immigrants have married into the elite, particularly since the 1940s. Surprisingly, given the strong presence of indigenous Ecuadorians in the highlands, Quito, Santo Domingo, and the Amazon region, only around 7 percent of Ecuadorians describe themselves as indigenous. There are some twenty-seven indigenous groups in the country, including the Andean Quichua and Amazonian Kichwa, who both speak Quechua, the *lingua franca* of the Inca empire. The Cofán, Siona, Tetete, Secoya, Waorani, Shuar, Achuar–Shiwiar, and Záparo are found in the Amazon areas of El Oriente, and the Cha'palaachi (Cayapa), Tsachila (Colorado), and Awa

An indigenous highlander in Chimbarazo Province, the central Andes.

indigenous groups are located in the coastal lowlands. Around 7 percent of Ecuadorians describe themselves as Montubios, a word used for the mixed-race people who live outside the main towns and cities along the coast, and another 7 percent describe themselves as Afro–Ecuadorian. These are largely descendants of slaves from

Africa who were concentrated in two areas: Esmeraldas
Province on the coast and the Chota valley in Imbabura
Province. In 2015, the traditional Marimba music, chants,
and dances from the Afro-Ecuadorian communities of
Esmeraldas Province was added to UNESCO's list of
Intangible Cultural Heritage of Humanity.

There are large communities of Colombians living
along the northern border and in Santo Domingo de los
Tsachilas, Peruvians in the south, and a small number
of Cubans in the main towns and cities. More recently,
there has been a significant influx of more than 400,000
Venezuelans who began to flood into Ecuador in 2017 to
escape political repression and a failed economy at home.

There is also a small but significant Lebanese
community. Known locally as *Turcos* (Turks), because
they first arrived at the end of the nineteenth century
when Lebanon was part of the Ottoman Empire, they
have provided the country with three presidents,
including Abdalá Bucaram and Jamil Mahuad. A four-
thousand-strong Jewish community, based mainly in
Quito and Guayaquil, dates from the 1930s, when Jews
fleeing persecution in Nazi Germany took shelter here.

CLIMATE

Despite its position on the Equator, Ecuador does not
have typically tropical weather throughout the country as
the climate depends on altitude. In the Sierra, the intermontane valleys enjoy a year-round spring, while in high
mountain villages nights can dip below freezing. It's easy

to get sunburned in Quito, even when the days are cloudy, due to the altitude. The coast is hot, and the jungles of Oriente are hot and humid.

Rainfall depends on the season. The dry season (*temporada seca*) is also known as *verano* (summer) and the rainy season (*temporada de lluvia*) is also known as *invierno* (winter). However, seasonal variations in rainfall depend on the region. In the Sierra, the rainy season generally runs from October to April. However, the weather is never predictable, and citizens of the Sierra say you can experience four seasons in one day in the mountains. Even in the dry season you should pack for the occasional shower or cold spell.

In the rainforests of the Oriente, high rainfall and humidity are the norm and there is little change in temperature throughout the year, although nights can get very cool. The rainy season is generally from April to September, but it can rain on any day.

The coastal area around Guayaquil can get very hot and humid in the rainy season from December to May. Esmeraldas in the north receives more rainfall than the southern coast, and the central coast is sometimes blanketed in a thick, damp mist, known as *garúa*.

In the Galápagos, the cooler dry season runs from July through December and is also known as the *garúa* season, with mist coming down from the higher elevations to the coast. Strangely, in the warm, wetter season from January to June there is very little rainfall on the low-lying coasts of the islands, and sunshine and blue skies are typical. Temperatures on the beaches range between 84°F (29°C) and 59°F (15°C).

THE EQUATORIAL BULGE AND DARWIN'S FINCHES

Ecuador provided the world with some major scientific breakthroughs in the eighteenth and nineteenth centuries, one of which gave the country its modern name. In 1735, the French Geodesic Mission traveled to South America to find out if the Earth was round or if it bulged out at the middle, a theory put forward by the English physicist Sir Isaac Newton (1643–1727). Led by the French mathematician and naturalist Charles Marie de La Condamine (1701–74), the mission planned to measure degrees of latitude on the Equator and compare them to measurements taken in Europe and the Arctic. Planned for three years, the expedition lasted nearly ten. Along the way, the scientists were exposed to extreme cold, and fevers, and the expedition's surgeon, Jean Seniergues, was stabbed to death by a mob at a Cuenca bullfight.

However, by triangulating the Andean peaks near Quito along a 215-mile line to the city of Cuenca, the French scientists established that one degree of latitude was shorter at the Equator, proving Newton's theory. Their discovery led to the production of the first accurate maps. It was La Condamine's adventure-filled account of his travels that associated the Audiencia de Quito with the "Land of the Equator" and led to the new republic being named Ecuador in 1830.

Inspired by the French expedition, the Prussian naturalist and explorer Alexander von Humboldt (1769–1859) arrived in Quito in 1802. A keen geologist and climber, he attempted to reach the snow-capped summit of Chimborazo, but only reached 19,286 feet (5,878 m) before yielding to altitude sickness. It wasn't until 1880 when the British climber Edward Whymper made it to the summit that Chimborazo was finally conquered. Humboldt dubbed the mountainous area around Chimborazo "the Avenue of the Volcanoes" and marveled that "Ecuadorians sleep peacefully amid smoking volcanoes, live in poverty atop riches, and are made happy by sad music."

On September 15, 1835, the British naturalist Charles Darwin (1809–82) arrived in the Galápagos Islands on HMS *Beagle*. He was immediately struck by the tameness of the local wildlife, and during the five weeks that he studied the archipelago he noted differences between the plants and animals on islands so close to each other. But it was only later, after much study of the collections he made there, that he came to the realization that the differences among the many finches he found on the islands were adaptations to different conditions over time. His short visit would lead, years later, to his groundbreaking book *On the Origin of Species*, the basis for the modern Theory of Evolution.

A BRIEF HISTORY

There is insufficient space to do full justice to the epic
sweep of Ecuador's pre-Columbian past and its complex
history, including as it does the blood-soaked struggle
of Atahualpa for control of the Inca empire; the brutal
Spanish conquest that brought a forced conversion
of the indigenous population to the Roman Catholic
religion; and the wars of independence that led to the
birth of Ecuador as a nation. Those momentous events
were followed in the nineteenth century by an internal
battle for control between Quito and Guayaquil, and a
largely unsuccessful external battle to protect the borders
from the depredations of the country's more powerful
neighbors Colombia and Peru. On the cusp of the twenty-
first century there was more turmoil, with indigenous
uprisings as an oppressed underclass took to the streets
to express their demands for a more inclusive and equal
society; military coups as the generals asserted their
will; and political upheaval as presidents failed to finish
their terms. After a ten-year period of relative political
stability and economic development under President
Rafael Correa, in 2017 the country slipped back into an
economic slump and social tensions have again increased
as indigenous groups struggle to make their voices heard.

The following is a brief summary of some of the key
events in the country's history.

Earliest People
The long-held theory that hunter-gatherers from Siberia
populated the Americas after crossing the Bering Strait

at the end of the last Ice Age, around 11,500 years ago, has been largely revised. Human footprints preserved in volcanic ash in Valsequillo, Mexico, date back 35,000 years and other archeological finds suggest even earlier dates. Recent DNA research indicates that the Americas were populated in several waves of migration over many years, and some of the first Americans probably used small boats to travel down the Pacific coast.

In Ecuador, the earliest known settlements belonged to the Las Vegas culture, which occupied several sites along the coast in present-day Santa Elena some 10,000 years ago. They subsisted on hunting, fishing, and foraging, and there is evidence in Santa Elena of the earliest examples of cultivated plants, such as the gourd tree and maize. The most dramatic discovery in the region was a cemetery of about two hundred burials, including a grave in which two skeletons were found in what looks like a tender embrace. Dubbed "*los Amantes de Sumpa*" (the Lovers of Sumpa), they are a major draw to a small museum built on the site.

The Valdivia Culture group (3,500–500 BCE) is the oldest ceramic civilization found in Ecuador, and are known for "Venus" or "Earth Mother" figurines, depicting naked, sometimes pregnant, women. Often intentionally broken, they may have been used in fertility and healing rituals. In the 1960s, Ecuadorian archeologist Emilio Estrada noticed strong similarities between the ceramics of Valdivia and the Jomon culture of Kyushu Island in Japan. Estrada's theory that Japanese fishermen had "discovered" the Americas four thousand years before Columbus was backed by US archeologist Betty Meggers, but is no longer seen as credible.

A jaguar figurine of the Valdivia Culture group, Ecuador's oldest cermaic culture.

Other important formative cultures include the Machalila (1,500–1,000 BCE) from Manabí and Santa Elena, who practiced cranial deformation in childhood, perhaps to identify an elite class; and the Chorrera (1,300–300 BCE), who made fine red pottery and used the shell of the *spondylus* (thorny oyster) as a form of currency to trade with other groups. La Tolita (600 BCE–400 CE), focused principally around Tolita Island in Esmeraldas, is named after the *tolas* (burial mounds) found here. A center for religious ceremonies possibly linked

A fragment of a human effigy produced by the Chorrera.

to ancestor worship, the island was home to artisans producing exquisite figurines and masks made of gold and platinum. The gold funerary mask of the Sun God in the Museo Nacional del Banco Central de Ecuador (Central Bank of Ecuador Museum) in Quito comes from Tolita.

Life Before the Incas

Before the arrival of the Incas, the Manteños, and the Caras, or Caranqui, were large tribal groups that emerged on the coast. The Caras built an impressive ceremonial site at Cochasqui, with fifteen large earth pyramids, that dates back to about 850 CE and continues to awe visitors today. Remains of hilltop fortresses called *pucaras* have also been excavated. Later, the Caras merged with the Quitus from the highlands to create a tribal confederation known as the Shyris. It was the Quitus who gave their name to Quito, a city named by the Incas. Another group that had extensive trade routes between the coast and the sea was the Yumbos, whose ceremonial site at Tulipe, in the cloud forests outside Quito, is only being slowly revealed by archeologists today. Other groups named by the Spanish chroniclers were the Puruhá, and the fierce Cañari in the south of the country. The Cañari were among the first of these large groups to come up against the armies of the famous Inca ruler Tupac Yupanqui. The Incas built Tomebamba (present-day Cuenca) on the site of an important Cañari community, and visitors to Ingapirca, the best-preserved Inca ruin in Ecuador, can still see the Cañari structures incorporated into the sun temple the Incas built on top of it.

The Arrival of the Incas

The Incas traced their history back to Manco Capac, a semi-mythical figure who was said to have emerged from a cave in 1070, but expansion from Cuzco, the Inca heartland, didn't pick up until the reign of Viracocha Pachacutec (ruled 1438–71), who conquered the rival Chimu Empire. It was his successor, Tupac Yupanqui (1471–93), who greatly expanded the empire to the south and north, including southern parts of present-day Ecuador. It was no easy conquest. The Incas' northern advance was held up for more than fifteen years by fierce resistance from the Caras, but under Huayna Capac (1493–1527), who was born in Tomebamba (present-day Cuenca), the Caras were finally defeated. The last major battle saw a victory for the Incas by the small lake of Yaguarcocha, north of Ibarra. This Quechua name means "Lake of Blood," and legend has it that thousands of Caranqui warriors and young men were killed here and its waters turned red by the spilled blood.

With the suppression of the Caras, the Incas stopped their advance at the present-day border with Colombia and set about consolidating their rule, imposing the worship of their Gods Inti and Viracocha, organizing the local tribes in line with their hierarchical structure, and building terraced fields and roads.

Life Under the Incas

The Inca Empire was the largest and most sophisticated pre-Columbian civilization in South America. At its height, just before the Spanish conquest, the Inca ruled over some 12 million people and controlled a territory that stretched about 1,500 miles (over 2,400 km) along the Andes from the border of present-day Colombia all the way south to the Maule River in central Chile.

At the top was the Sapa Inca, the emperor, an absolute ruler who was considered a divine being directly descended from the Sun God Inti. The royal crown was a fringe of red tassels worn across the forehead. He had complete control over an aristocratic bureaucracy of nobles and chiefs that, in turn, managed a caste system in which the vast bulk of the population lived like serfs.

As new territories were conquered the Inca would impose control by adding an Inca noble at the head of the existing tribal structure. The Inca language, Quechua, was also imposed on subject people, and Viracocha was installed as the Creator God. Rebellious tribes were relocated to another part of the empire, and pro-Inca tribes were sent in to replace them. The system was hugely successful. Ecuador was only under Inca rule for some forty years before the arrival of the Spanish, but Quechua is still the language spoken by the largest indigenous groups today.

There was no currency or money. Serfs paid taxes in the form of labor, such as working in the fields of the emperor, in return for land they could work themselves. Surplus food was stored, and released to feed the people in times of poor harvests, or to feed the old and sick. It also went to feed the huge Inca army as it patrolled the empire, and laborers working on communal tasks like building palaces, fortresses, and the thousands of miles of roads that were used for trade and by the army. There were strict rules on what people at different levels of society could eat and what they could wear, and fine textiles made of the fibers from vicuña, alpaca, and guanaco—all valuable animals—were restricted to those at the top.

The Incas didn't invent the wheel, so all transport was by foot, with llamas domesticated as pack animals. Important messages were sent by *chasqui* runners. Their job was made harder by the fact that there was no writing; instead, the Inca used arrangements of knotted colored strings called *quipus* to keep records or inventories. The key to the meaning of the *quipus* died with the Inca elite in the Spanish conquest, so archeologists today can only guess at their use.

Inca religion was based on ancestor worship and the mummification of past Incas and nobles. A caste of priests presided over ceremonies offering maize and *chicha* (drink, typically made from maize) to Gods such as Inti (the Sun), Viracocha (the Creator), Illya'pa (the Rain), Mama Kilya (the Moon), Pacha Mama (the Earth), Mama Coca (the Sea), and Mama Sara (Maize). The Inca also sacrificed guinea pigs, llamas, and, more rarely, young women and children, before major events like going to war.

Rituals were linked to an agricultural calendar and sacred sites, known as *huacas,* which could be man-made temples or natural features such as sacred rocks, waterfalls, rivers, and mountains (still revered as *Apus,* or lords, by Quechua-speakers in Ecuador's highlands today).

The Inca heartland was focused around the capital, Cuzco, a name that means "navel" in Quechua. This was a sacred city to the Incas, and at its center was the resplendent Coricancha temple, decorated throughout with gold panels and gold offerings to the Sun God, Inti. From the central plaza four main roads radiated out to the four corners of the empire: Cuntisuyo covered Cuzco to the Pacific coast, Antisuyo to the southwest, Collasuyo in the south extending into Chile and Argentina, and Chinchasuya in the north, covering present-day Ecuador.

Plague, Fever, and Decline

When Francisco Pizarro landed in Tumbes in 1532 with his tiny army of 106 foot soldiers and sixty-two horsemen, the mighty Inca Empire had already been decimated by a deadly disease from the north. Huayna Capac had only finished subjugating the warlike tribes of present-day Ecuador when he was alerted by *chasqui* runners of a plague heading toward Quito. Those afflicted suffered skin eruptions all over the body, provoking fevers, agony, and death. It is now believed that the plague, which arrived in the New World with Christopher Columbus, was smallpox, against which the native population of the Americas had no natural defenses.

A portrait of Spanish conquistador Francisco Pizarro by French painter Amable-Paul Coutan.

33

Huayna Capac was himself struck down in 1527, dying shortly after learning of another great threat to the empire: the arrival of bearded foreigners who rode on strange beasts and carried sticks that spoke like thunder and killed from afar.

Pizarro's arrival couldn't have come at a worse time for the Incas. In Ecuador, Huayna Capac had fathered a son called Atahualpa with a Cara princess, Paccha Duchicela, from Caranqui. After his father's death Atahualpa fought his half-brother Huascar in a bloody civil war that pitted the armies of Quito against the armies of Cuzco and saw local tribes take sides. The war ended with the triumph of Atahualpa, but he had little time to savor his victory. Before he could have Huascar executed and consolidate his position he learned that Francisco Pizarro was on his way to Cajamarca to meet him; instead of sending an army he gave way to curiosity and agreed to come and see the strangers.

Atahualpa Meets Pizarro: Two Worlds Collide

The epoch-changing meeting between Atahualpa and Pizarro on November 16, 1532, is one of the key events in the Spanish conquest of Latin America. The Spanish numbered only 168 and faced a battle-hardened Inca army numbering many tens of thousands, but they had the advantage of steel swords and armor, horses, cannons, and a few harquebuses (small-caliber long guns). Inca warriors wore only cotton vests and wielded wooden clubs, spears, and wooden swords tipped with obsidian (volcanic glass).

Atahualpa arrived at the meeting with Pizarro with great pomp, carried aloft on a litter by attendants decked out in magnificent tunics with gold and silver ornaments glinting

ATAHUALLPA. INCA XIIII.

A depiction of Atahualpa by an unknown artist of the Cusco School.

in the sun, and followed by a procession of some five thousand unarmed men. While the conquistadors lay in wait, Friar Vicente de Valverde approached the Inca ruler with a bible and a cross and asked Atahualpa, through an interpreter, to accept Charles V as his sovereign and to convert to the Catholic religion. Atahualpa, unused to a writing system, held up the bible to his ear to hear the great words the friar had spoken of and then cast it down to the ground, angry at the friar's words. Pizarro then forced his way through the throng to the Inca, grabbed his arm, and pulled him from the litter crying "Santiago!"—the call for the cavalry to charge and the cannons to fire into the massed Inca warriors. Trapped in the square, the panicked Incans were easy prey for the better-armed Spaniards. Within an hour Pizarro had captured Atahualpa and killed five thousand of his troops and retainers. The only injury on the Spanish side was a cut to Pizarro's hand.

Atahualpa, thinking he could escape captivity by giving the foreigners the precious metals they so coveted, offered to fill one room with gold and another with silver in return for his freedom. Pizarro agreed, but before the rooms had been completely filled he realized that Atahualpa was a liability to his plans for conquest. After the defeated Inca Huascar was murdered on Atahualpa's orders while being brought to Cajamarca, Pizarro charged Atahualpa with idolatry and treason, and ordered that he should be burned at the stake. In the end, on August 29, 1533, Atahualpa was "shown mercy" and garotted (strangled)—an important difference to the Incas, who mummified the bodies of their dead rulers. Pizarro, with the aid of disaffected tribes like the Cañari, then began to consolidate his control over the Inca Empire.

The last great hurrah of Atahualpa's army came with General Rumiñahui, who hid in the Llanganates mountains a huge treasure of gold he was bringing to Cajamarca for Atahualpa's release. Rumiñahui was eventually captured and executed, but not before he had engaged the Spaniards in several battles and burned the Inca city of Quito to the ground. Despite cruel tortures, Rumiñahui never gave away the location of the Llanganates gold, and treasure hunters seek it to this day.

Life Under the Spanish

The present city of Quito was founded by Sebastian de Benalcazar on December 6, 1534. Francisco de Pizarro's brother, Gonzalo, became the first governor of the city in 1541, and started building the plazas, churches, and government buildings that made it one of the finest cities in the Spanish Americas. The religious conversion of the locals was a key goal, as was the construction of churches on top of local sites of worship, to stamp out "heathen" beliefs. The indigenous people not only had to learn a new religion, but they had the backbreaking task of building the twenty churches and convents that rose up in Quito from the ruins of the Inca city. Local craftsmen were taught the artistic techniques that were needed to fill all these palaces of worship with devotional images and statues, creating the famous *Escuela Quiteña* (School of Quito) that by the seventeenth and eighteenth centuries was famous for supplying unrivaled religious artworks to churches and convents all over South and Central America.

From the outset, the Audiencia Real de Quito (Royal Audience of Quito), an administrative unit encompassing much of present-day Ecuador, was fought over by its two more powerful neighbors. Established in 1563, it initially came under the control of the Viceroyalty of Peru, but in 1717 it was transferred to the administration of the Viceroyalty of New Granada (covering present-day Colombia).

The indigenous people and the lands they inhabited were shared out among the Spanish in a system known as *encomiendas*. Ironically, the Inca hierarchy that was already in place helped the small number of Spanish conquistadors to exercise control over vast lands, and they quickly introduced new agricultural projects, from cattle herding to the growing of wheat and bananas. The only difference from Inca rule was that the Spanish worked the people harder and gave them less in return. They also took and shared among them the Inca nobles' most beautiful wives and concubines, starting the process of *mestizaje* (racial mixing) that took place across the Spanish Americas.

AMAZON ADVENTURERS

Ecuadorians will tell you that Ecuador is an Amazonian country, a concept that has led to conflict with neighboring Peru on several occasions and is still a bone of contention. The roots of this strongly held conviction date back to February 1541, when a large expedition set out from Quito, led by Gonzalo Pizarro, to find *El Dorado* (the "Golden One"). Gonzalo sought not only a gilded ruler with riches reputedly greater than the Incas, but also a lost land blessed with cinnamon trees, whose bark provided a spice highly coveted in Spain. Instead, he got lost. His second-in-command, Francisco de Orellana (1511–46), found his way down the mighty river, after setting off in search of food and never returning. One hostile tribe that Orellana found was made up of warrior women who showered their boats with arrows, like the Amazons of Greek myth. The expedition's priest, Fray Carvajal, therefore called the river "Rio de las Amazonas"— a name that stuck.

Orellana was the first European to travel the length of the Amazon, and his name lives on in El Oriente, where the starting point of his journey on the Rio Napo is called Puerto Francisco de Orellana, although most locals call it Coca.

Two hundred years later, on October 1, 1769, a young woman from Riobamba, Isabel Godin,

set out down the Amazon bound for French
Guiana to rejoin her husband, who had been part
of the French scientific expedition led by Charles
Marie de La Condamine. Her remarkable tale of
jungle survival is engagingly recounted in Robert
Whitaker's book *The Mapmaker's Wife*.

The Move to Independence

There were several indigenous uprisings in the Audience of
Quito in response to the harsh conditions of Spanish rule,
but it was not until the end of the eighteenth century that a
broad independence movement began to take shape.

The *encomiendas* had given way to an equally brutal
system known as *huasipungo*, in which agricultural
workers were treated as powerless serfs slaving away for
their rich Spanish masters. African slaves had also been
brought over to work sugar plantations in the Chota
Valley, but not in great numbers, and slaves shipwrecked
in 1535 had created their own settlements in Esmeraldas.

A rigid caste system operated under the Spanish that
placed the indigenous inhabitants at the bottom of society,
mestizos in the lower and middle ranks, and a small ruling
class made up of the descendants of Spanish settlers,
known as *criollos* (creoles). The top jobs were given to
peninsulares, the Spanish-born officials who oversaw the
colonial administration and controlled trade.

On August 10, 1809, a group of *criollos* led by Juan
Pío Montúfar rose up in Quito to denounce Napoleon's
invasion of Spain. The French emperor had forced
Charles IV and his son, Ferdinand VII, to abdicate,

and placed his own brother on the Spanish throne as Joseph I. The *criollos* were not at this stage calling for full independence, but for the restoration of the Spanish king. After twenty-four days Spanish troops regained control and the conspirators jailed. Ten of them were later hacked to death by their guards after a failed rescue attempt.

The momentum had started, however, and Quito to this day is known as the "Luz de America" (Light of America) for its part in inspiring other Latin Americans to fight for their independence.

Independence Gained

Another revolutionary government was formed in 1810 that lasted until 1812, but it was not until October 9, 1820, when Guayaquil proclaimed its independence from Spain in a bloodless revolt and set up a revolutionary junta, that Spanish control in the region was seriously challenged.

Meanwhile, the Venezuelan independence fighter Simón Bolívar (1783–1830) had effectively defeated the Spanish royalists at the Battle of Boyacá in August 1819 and brought his army down south to support Guayaquil. Bolívar's lover was the Quito-born Manuela Saenz (1795–1856), whom he called *La Libertadora del Libertador* (The Liberator's Liberator), for saving his life in Bogotá. A bronze statue of her in full military dress, sword in hand, stands outside the Mitad del Mundo near Quito, and her house has been converted into a small museum.

On May 24, 1822, Bolívar's most trusted general, Antonio José de Sucre (1795–1830), led the independence forces to victory at the Battle of Pichincha, finally liberating Quito from Spanish rule.

Back in Guayaquil in July, Bolívar had a famous meeting with another great South American independence hero, José de San Martín (1778–1850), who had defeated the Spanish in Argentina, Chile, and most of Peru, and who also wanted to liberate Ecuador. Trumped by a triumphant Bolívar, a despondent and exhausted San Martín surrendered the glory of the decisive battle to free Peru to Bolívar, which took place on December 9, 1824, at the Battle of Ayacucho.

What had been the Audiencia de Quito now became the Departamento del Sur (Southern Department) of Gran Colombia, joining present-day Venezuela, Colombia, Panama, Peru, and Bolivia (named in honor of Simón Bolívar) under one flag.

A New Nation Emerges From Gran Colombia

Simón Bolívar's dream of a federation of Colombian nations did not last long. Venezuela broke away from Gran Colombia on May 13, 1830, and the Departamento del Sur soon followed suit. The name chosen for this new republic was Ecuador, a compromise to the political factions from Guayaquil who preferred the rather insipid Republic of the Equator (a literal translation) to using the name Quito for the whole county, as it had been under Spanish rule. The first president of the new nation was a Venezuelan independence fighter, Juan José Flores (1800–64), who had married into the Quito elite. Known as the "Father of the Republic," Flores had to contend with many forces trying to tear the fledgling nation apart, and was exiled in 1845 after an uprising in Guayaquil of a group known as the *Marcistas*. Later, another group in Guayaquil ceded part of the country to a Peruvian invasion force in a virtual civil war that ended only when Flores won the Battle of Guayaquil in September 1860.

The rivalry between Quito and Guayaquil hardened into a political battle between the Liberals on the coast and the Conservatives in the highlands from the 1860s onwards. The Conservative President Gabriel García Moreno (1821–75) was staunchly Catholic, and handed the power for education to the Church, which made him unpopular, especially with the Freemasons. On August 6, 1875, he was hacked to death with a machete on the steps of the Presidential Palace. A plaque on the wall records his last words, "*Dios no muere!*" (God does not die!)

The violence continued into the twentieth century, when Liberal President Eloy Alfaro was murdered in 1912. Alfaro undid Moreno's reforms by secularizing education and legalizing divorce. He also finished the Quito-to-Guayaquil Trans-Andean railway, finally linking the highlands with the coast. Ironically, he was arrested in Guayaquil for his part in a coup plot and taken back by rail to Quito, where he was seized by a Catholic mob, dragged through the streets, and murdered, his body burned to ashes in the present-day Parque El Ejido.

Military Rule, Invasion, and Oil Boom

The period from the 1920s to the 1970s saw Ecuador transformed from a major exporter of cacao (cocoa beans) to a real-life banana republic and, finally, an oil exporter. The 1960s also saw a change to the laws that kept peasant farmers tied to the plantations in conditions akin to slavery.

In the political sphere, instability was the norm, with the military ousting governments on a whim as they amassed more power. A great populist and eloquent speechmaker, José María Velasco Ibarra (1893–1979), used to say "Give me a balcony and I will become president." True to his word, he was elected president five times between 1934 and 1968, but only once finished his term, the other four times being deposed in military coups.

The period also saw the greatest loss of Ecuadorian territory, when in 1941 fighting broke out between Ecuador and Peru over Ecuador's Amazonian territory. The Peruvian army vastly outnumbered the Ecuadorian troops on the border and even dropped paratroopers into Ecuador, eventually occupying parts of Loja, El Oro Province, and the Amazon. The resulting peace treaty of 1942, known as the Rio Protocol, gave some 77,000 square miles of territory to Peru and left another 38,000 square miles open to dispute because of a lack of clarity over the new borders. Later Ecuadorian governments have challenged the protocol, arguing that it was signed under duress by a military junta while Peru occupied Ecuadorian territory. Tensions continued to simmer, especially in the Cordillera del Condor, which finally erupted in January 1981 in a brief military conflict known as the Paquisha War. In January 1995 there was a short but bitter clash between the two nations over outposts on the Cenepa River that led to aerial bombing by both sides. A final resolution of the dispute was reached on October 26, 1998, brokered by Brazil, and signed by Ecuadorian President Jamil Mahuad and his Peruvian counterpart Alberto Fujimori.

Political Turmoil, Economic Meltdown, and Dollarization

The 1990s saw further political upheaval with the election in 1996 of the Guayaquil populist Abdala Bucaram, who ran his political rallies like product launches, with music, dancing, and giveaways. After promising electors a prosperous future, it soon became apparent that he was more interested in partying than steadying the spiraling inflation that was forcing up prices. Leading the opposition to Bucaram was the Confederation of Indigenous Nationalities of Ecuador (CONAIE), which for the first time brought indigenous issues to the forefront in politics. Strikes and street protests eventually brought down Bucaram, known as "El Loco" (the Madman), who was declared "mentally unfit" by Congress and skipped the country, in an unprecedented scenario that saw three presidents in three days. Then, in 1998, the country was struck by El Niño, a weather phenomenon that whipped up storms and floods, devastating the coast and badly affecting the fishing and shrimp industries. President Jamil Mahuad, faced by falling oil prices, inflation of 60 percent, rising unemployment, a bank bailout, and a freeze on bank deposits, decided in 1999 to take the drastic step of replacing the nation's currency, the sucre, with the US dollar. The decision provoked mass strikes and protests by the trade unions and CONAIE against the deeply unpopular president. Mahuad was forced to resign on January 21, 2000, when the capital was besieged by indigenous protesters supported by Colonel Lucio Gutiérrez and his troops. This short-term coup did not stop dollarization, which was passed by President

Gustavo Noboa in September 2000, destroying the savings and purchasing power of ordinary Ecuadorians overnight and creating a massive surge in migration to Spain, the United States, and Italy.

Gutiérrez was elected president in 2002 on a populist platform supported by indigenous groups who expected him to bring in social policies favoring the poor. Instead, he brought in an IMF-sponsored austerity package, prompting a week of mass protests that led the army to withdraw their support for his government and a Congressional vote to oust him. After three presidents were ousted in less than ten years, in 2006 young economist Rafael Correa (born 1963), was elected president, ushering in an extended period of political stability that saw economic advances, a rise in the standard of living, and a reduction in poverty and illiteracy. A committed Christian and a declared socialist, Correa benefited from high prices for Ecuador's crude oil exports and used the income to invest in social policies and infrastructure projects. Critics argued that the government indebted the country to China to the tune of billions of dollars in return for future oil

President Rafael Correa during a national military parade, Quito, 2012.

sales and the increasing involvement of Chinese oil and mineral companies in Ecuador.

When President Correa's former vice-president and anointed successor, Lenin Moreno, became president in 2017, it was believed that the wheelchair-bound politician would continue Correa's socialist policies. Instead he broke away from the path forged by his former leader; he let the US make use of a military runway in the Galápagos Islands, revoked Wikileaks founder Julian Assange's asylum in the Ecuadorian Embassy in London, secured a US $6.5 billion loan from the IMF, and removed fuel subsidies, which prompted nationwide protests until the subsidies were restored. Meanwhile, corruption charges brought against Correa forced him into virtual exile in Belgium, rendering him unable to participate in politics.

By the elections of 2021, Moreno's popularity rating was at a dismal 7 percent—the economy had contracted by nearly 7 percent in one year, and the government's handling of the Covid-19 pandemic was characterized as one of the worst in Latin America after Brazil. Moreno's shortcomings led to the subsequent presidential victory of Guillermo Lasso, a millionaire banker who hopes to reverse stagnation by means of a market-oriented overhaul of the country's economy.

GOVERNMENT

Ecuador is a Democratic Republic with a president, elected by universal suffrage every four years, who is both head of state and head of government, and has the power to appoint the vice president and a cabinet of ministers. Over its history Ecuador has been one of the least stable republics in South America, with nearly one hundred governments and twenty constitutions since it declared itself independent from Gran Colombia in 1830.

The legislative branch consists of a unicameral Asamblea Nacional (National Assembly) of 137 deputies who are elected every four years concurrently with presidential elections. The National Assembly has the power to pass laws.

Under the 2008 Constitution the right to vote was extended to police officers, military personnel, and prisoners. It also extended the vote to sixteen- and seventeen-year-olds, on an optional basis, while for eighteen- to sixty-five-year-olds voting is compulsory.

The appointment of judges to the National Court of Justice is carried out by a separate Council of the Judiciary, created after a constitutional amendment was approved in a national referendum held in 2011.

Local government is administered by the governors of the country's twenty-four provinces. The provincial administrations are run by a governor chosen by the president, and a prefect (*prefecto*) and provincial government (*gobierno provincial*) elected by popular vote. The 221 cantons that are subdivisions of the provinces are run by a representative of the president, and a mayor (*alcalde*) and a municipal council (*concejo municipal*) elected by popular vote.

OIL AND THE ENVIRONMENT

Ecuador's most important source of foreign earnings comes from crude oil, but a long history of oil spills has left a toxic legacy of contamination in the jungles of El Oriente, where most of the country's oil reserves are located.

Oil exploration in El Oriente began in 1937, when Royal Dutch Shell was offered a concession, but production didn't start until 1964 when Texaco began operations. By 1970, Texaco had completed the Trans-Andean Pipeline bringing crude oil from Lago Agrio to Esmeraldas on the coast. Given the volcanic nature of the region, there have been significant oil spills over the years, including the release of 420,000 gallons (1.6 million liters) of crude oil into the Napo River in 2013 that contaminated the river all the way to downstream Peru and Brazil.

Worse, between 1964 and 1990 Texaco was accused of contaminating an area of 1,700 square miles (4,400 sq. km) that is home to the Cofan, Sicoya, and Huarani indigenous groups with 18 billion gallons (68 billion liters) of toxic wastewater and 17 million gallons (64 billion liters) of crude oil. Chevron, which merged with Texaco in 2001, is still fighting against the damages awarded to the affected indigenous groups by an Ecuadorian court in February 2013.

In April 2020, the rupture of three pipelines created a major oil spill in the Napo and Coca rivers that directly affected 105 forest communities, the cleanup of which has, at the time of writing, yet to get underway. Despite publicly expressing concern at opening up the vast protected rainforest of the Parque Nacional Yasuní to oil exploration, in 2021 President Guillermo Lasso pledged to boost oil production and increase mining output, prompting fears of further environmental crises in the Amazon region.

THE ECONOMY

Crude oil may be king, but Ecuador's economic development in the past was tied principally to the agricultural production of potatoes, wheat, and maize, and cash crops for export such as coffee, cacao (cocoa beans), sugar cane, and bananas. Cocoa beans, cultivated since colonial times, were the main generator of foreign earnings from the nineteenth century until the 1920s, when local blight and foreign competition hit exports. The cocoa business is now bouncing back as the international demand for premium chocolate has seen local producers like Pacari make the most of the country's fine aromatic cocoa beans, known as "Nacional" or "Arriba," which international connoisseurs consider the best kind of *forastero* beans.

The next big crop was bananas. Native to Asia and taken to Africa in ancient times, the first bananas to arrive in the New World came with the Spanish

Conquistadors, who brought them from the Canary Islands. Fray Tomás de Berlanga, who brought the first banana cuttings to Hispaniola in 1516, was the first person to describe the Galápagos Islands in 1535. Today, Ecuador is the number one banana exporter in the world, shipping out some five million bananas annually. The industry began quite modestly in 1910, and it was the huge post-Second World War boom in banana consumption in Europe and the US that gave Ecuador the boost it needed. By 1952 it had surpassed Central America in exports.

Exports of cut flowers have also experienced significant growth in the last twenty years. Ecuador has the advantage of year-round spring-like weather that is perfect for growing roses. Equatorial roses are famous for having straighter, thicker, and longer stems due to the overhead sun. Ecuador exports about $600 million of cut flowers a year to its main export markets in the US, Italy, and Russia, supplying organic and fair-trade flowers to an increasingly discerning public.

Large-scale oil production began in 1972 in the northern Oriente and provides over half of the government's earnings. As described above, oil extraction also constitutes the country's main environmental dilemmas. The smallest oil producer in the Organization of Petroleum Exporting Countries (OPEC), Ecuador exports more than a third of its oil to the US but has been trying to increase the amount it supplies to Russia and China. Oil revenue is offset by the lack of refining capacity, which means gasoline still has to be imported. Ecuador is also looking to exploit other natural resources, including the gas deposits in the Gulf of Guayaquil, and an estimated $2 billion of gold reserves. Remittances—the money sent back by Ecuadorians working abroad in Spain, the US, Italy, the UK, and elsewhere—is the second-biggest source of foreign revenue after oil.

The trauma of dollarization in 2000, which sparked a mass exodus of Ecuadorian migrants, has now helped to stabilize the economy. It has also helped to attract growing numbers of retirees from the US who in turn have further boosted the economy. These expat retirees are mainly located in Cuenca, Vilcabamba, and towns along the coast.

Before the coronavirus pandemic, tourism was Ecuador's third largest non-oil sector after banana and shrimp. It ensured employment for thousands of people across the country and helped to bring income to indigenous communities in remote areas. The indusrty was completely devastated by the ensuing lockdowns and travel restrictions put in place around the world. At the time of writing, tourism to the historic cities of Quito and Cuenca, the ever-popular Galápagos Islands, and mainland beach resorts like Montañita, have begun to bounce back despite a lagging local vaccination program. No one expects that the recovery of the tourism sector will be quick, but people in the industry are hopeful and quietly confident that there will be a gradual return to pre-pandemic levels of visitors in the coming years as people adjust.

CHAPTER TWO

VALUES & ATTITUDES

THE FAMILY

Two generations ago many Ecuadorians came from very large families, with five to seven children being common in rural areas, and eight or nine not unusual. Today, the average family size is less than three children per couple across the country. Poor rural families tend to have more children than rich urban ones, although the financial pressures of raising a family in a city mean that low-income families in Quito and Guayaquil are also smaller.

Not surprisingly, the family is the most important unit in the life of Ecuadorians. Respect for elders and for the family is instilled at a young age. Typically, young children will ask their mother, father, uncles, or godparents for a blessing, with the words, *Bendición, tío* ("Blessing, uncle"), and will receive one, with the words, *Dios te bendiga, hijo* ("God bless you, child"). Grandparents, children, and grandchildren often live under one roof; brothers, sisters, aunts, uncles, and cousins often live nearby and keep in regular contact, helping each other out when the need arises.

People spend a great deal of time with their extended family. There is a constant round of parties and celebrations to cement family bonds, such as birthdays, marriages, christenings, *quinceañeras* (the fifteenth-birthday parties for girls), and Christmas and New Year festivities.

Rich or poor, grandparents or elderly relatives typically remain in the family house to be cared for by younger relatives rather than moving to an assisted-living facility or retirement community. Ecuadorians who have lived abroad sometimes comment on the "coldness" of people in the US or the UK, who tend to live in a nuclear family unit, spend little time with relatives, and are prepared to let others care for their elderly parents.

Children typically stay at home while they study at college or university, and leave the nest only after they marry. Men often wait to marry until they are in a financial position to start a home of their own, so thirty-something bachelors living with their parents are quite common. It's also not unusual to find single mothers living at home and relying on their parents to help bring up their children.

ATTITUDES TOWARD RELIGION

The dominant religious influence in Ecuador continues to be the Catholic Church, and more than 75 percent of the population define themselves as Roman Catholics. The strong presence of the Church is not surprising given the aggressive conversion of the indigenous population by Catholic priests which began in 1532 with the Spanish conquest. The Diocese of Quito was established as early as 1545. Under colonial rule, the Church had a virtual monopoly over worship and education, which continued until Ecuador became a secular state in 1899. If you had any doubts about the power of the Catholic religion in Ecuador, then take a quick stroll around the historic centers of Quito and Cuenca, where church after impressive church—each one decorated with huge gilded altars and religious artworks—reflects the opulent wealth of these institutions of moral instruction and social control.

For some, Catholicism is something they are born into rather than a devout calling—but baptisms, first communions, confirmations, weddings, and funerals are important milestones in people's lives. Even Ecuadorians who don't go to church will carry images of saints and virgins for "protection," or place a candle in front of a Catholic saint to say a prayer and ask a favor.

Up in the Sierra, Catholic rituals and indigenous beliefs have blended to create a syncretic form of folk Catholicism, where a prayer to the Virgin Mary may also invoke the Pachamama (the Inca Earth Goddess), or involve elements of shamanism. Catholic festivals and saints' days are not always so religious and may reflect indigenous customs and beliefs, especially in and around Otavalo in the highlands. Inti Raymi, the Inca festival of the Sun, was for centuries celebrated under the guise of the saints John, Peter, and Paul, with mask dancing, *tinku* (ritual fighting), and the drinking of copious amounts of alcoholic *chicha* (fermented maize)—see Chapter 3 for more.

Protestant and Evangelical church groups such as Southern Baptists, the Church of Jesus Christ of Latter-day Saints (Mormons), Jehovah's Witnesses, and others have made inroads in poor areas of the big cities, especially in Guayaquil, and in indigenous areas in the highlands. There are hundreds of these churches, and they minister to about 10 percent of the population.

ATTITUDES TOWARD DIVORCE AND ABORTION

In the Liberal Revolution of 1895, led by the anti-clerical Jose Eloy Alfaro (1842–1912), the state became secular and freedom of religion became law, with education becoming the responsibility of the state. Under these reforms, civil marriage superseded church marriage, and divorce became legal. Although initially frowned upon for eroding Catholic family values, attitudes to both marriage and divorce have become more relaxed in recent years. The Catholic Church's entrenched opposition to abortion, however, means that it is still illegal, except in cases where the life of the mother is threatened or, since 2021, where the pregnancy is the result of rape.

Sanctions are harsh, although seldom enforced, with a one- to five-year prison sentence for a woman who has an abortion and a two- to five-year prison sentence for the person who carries it out. Only some two hundred legal abortions are carried out each year in Ecuador, forcing many women to endanger their lives by turning to backstreet abortionists and risking harsh jail sentences. In its 2021 ruling on decriminalizing abortions of pregnancies resulting from rape, the Constitutional Court left the door open for the National Assembly to enact decriminalization in further circumstances, calling on the government to legislate in ways that fulfil the constitutional right to live with dignity.

LGBTQ IN ECUADOR

Homosexuality was decriminalized in 1997 and in 1998 Ecuador became the first country in Latin America to enshrine protection against discrimination based on sexual orientation or gender identity in the constitution. Despite pressure from the Catholic Church, civil unions for same-sex couples were recognized in 2014, and in 2019 same-sex marriages became legal after a landmark ruling by the Constitutional Court. Further change may be on the horizon: current President Guillermo Lasso, though a devout Catholic, has pledged to address LGBTQ issues in Ecuador as well as the issues of abortion and gender violence.

Overall, attitudes toward same-sex relationships have changed markedly in the last decade, with greater social acceptance of the LGBTQ community and their rights throughout the country. Smaller rural communities in the Andes and among some Catholic and Evangelical groups tend to hold more conservative views on homosexuality and gender identity, however.

A growing LGBTQ movement organizes annual Pride marches in Quito, Guayaquil, and other cities and in 2021, the lighting up of the Palacio de Carondelet with the rainbow Pride flag reflects just how far Ecuador has come on the issue and the community's standing in Ecuadorian society.

MEN, WOMEN, AND *MACHISMO*

Though things are slowly changing, many Ecuadorians— both men and women—still have an old-school approach to gender relations, whereby men are expected to be emotionally reserved and decision makers, while women are expected to keep quiet, look after their appearance, bring up the children, and keep the house in order.

The different treatment of boys and girls starts young. Boys are not usually expected to help with housework while young girls are expected to learn all the skills of running a home. In the current economic environment, in which both partners have to work to make ends meet, many women have to shoulder the burden of holding down a full-time job, while still looking after children and doing most of the cooking and cleaning at home. Visit a country market and the majority of the vendors will be women, many with a child strapped to their back with a blanket or shawl, and maybe other children helping out.

Many men in Ecuador continue to expect a traditional arrangement in the home and have been slower to adapt to the modern world of working women and shared responsibilities. They are still expected to make the first move in initiating romance, to pay for everything on dates, and to lead when dancing *cumbia*, *salsa*, and *merengue*. Despite this romantic side, some men in Ecuador still cling to the belief that their manliness is linked to how many mistresses they have and how many children they father, which leads to households where abandoned single women are left to bring up children on their own.

There was a time not so long ago when it was deemed inadmissible for a woman to give evidence against her husband. In recent years women's groups have made strides in fighting for greater protection for women, and there are now Family Courts that deal with abusive relationships. These courts can issue restraining orders, fine or imprison abusive partners, and forcibly remove them from the family home.

A UN report on women showed that the poorest, least educated, and hardest-working women in Ecuador were those who identified themselves as indigenous. They also had low rates of literacy. Moves to target these disadvantaged groups by the government have had some success in improving the situation, but huge disparities still exist between the lives of the rich elite, with their maids, nannies, and cooks, and the indigenous wives and mothers who toil away in the small towns and villages of the Sierra.

REGIONAL RIVALRY

You don't have to spend long in Ecuador to come across an example of the historic and deep-seated rivalry between Quito and Guayquil. More than just a grudge match between the country's two most important cities, the Quito–Guayaquil divide represents a geographic split of Ecuador into the highlands, with a large indigenous population and the country's seat of political power in Quito, and the coast, with a mainly *mestizo* population and the commercial center of the country in Guayaquil. As one observer noted, "Ecuador does its business in Guayaquil, its praying in Quito."

The debate between the two sides can get quite heated. Those from the highlands (known as Serranos because they live in the Sierra) call those from the coast *monos* (monkeys) and look down on them as being loud, brash, show-offs, and thieves. Those from the coast (known as Costeños) deride their Andean cousins for being slow, conservative, and hypocritical. Sometimes you hear Costeños describe people from the Sierra as *longos,* which is just another way of calling them "Indians."

To the outside observer, Serranos come across as polite, reserved, slightly stoic, fatalistic, and soft-spoken, like their Andean neighbors in Peru and Bolivia—which is not surprising, considering the linguistic and historic heritage shared by Quechua speakers of the highlands. Costeños live in a much warmer environment, speak fast, are more dynamic, love to dance *salsa*, and are more outgoing. There is also an economic element to the quarrel. Costeños claim that they make all the money while Serrano bureaucrats in Quito spend their days finding more ways to tax the hard-earned profits from the coastal banana and cocoa plantations and the port of Guayaquil, only to distribute the money around the Sierra.

There are even some in Guayaquil who see the independence hero Simon Bolívar as a traitor, because he put down a rebellion in the city and incorporated it into Gran Colombia when the locals wanted to go it alone or join Peru. It was pressure from Guayaquil that stopped the country taking the name Quito and opting for Ecuador instead. Later in the nineteenth century there was constant friction between the pro-Church Conservatives in Quito and the anti-clerical Liberals in Guayaquil, which further polarized the situation, saw politicians assassinated, and on several occasions brought the country close to civil war. Even today Quito and Guayaquil fight over which is the more important city—especially when there's a soccer match between the two regional rivals.

Friendly Insults

Ecuadorians are fond of giving friends and colleagues nicknames, often using the diminutive form of the adjective by adding -ito or -ita at the end. Friends or family member will happily greet a girl who's slim with a cheery *Hola, flaquita* ("Hey, skinny girl") or a girlfriend refer to her rotund boyfriend as *mi gordito* ("my little fatty"). Everything depends on the delivery and the tone of voice. If you are a foreign visitor to Ecuador and somebody addresses you as a *gringo* or *gringa* (used to describe somebody from the US), they are not necessarily being confrontational.

NATIONAL PRIDE

Ecuadorians are very proud of their small country and its national heroes. The sixteenth-century Inca general Rumiñahui, who was born in Pillaro in Tungurahua, is considered to be one of the country's first national heroes, especially by indigenous Ecuadorians, because he fought so valiantly against the Spanish after the death of Atahualpa and burnt the Inca city of Quito to the ground rather than let it fall into Spanish hands.

Another source of national pride is the yellow, blue, and red Ecuadorian flag, which, like the flags of Colombia and Venezuela, is based on a design by the Venezuelan general and revolutionary thinker Francisco de Miranda (1750–1816). The yellow stripe is double the thickness of the other two and symbolizes the abundance and fertility of the land. Blue symbolizes the sea and the sky, and red symbolizes the blood that was spilled in the fight for independence from Spain. The national coat of arms appears in the center. Topped by an Andean condor that offers its protection over the nation, it features the snow-covered cone of Mount Chimborazo and the Guayas River, which links the Sierra with the coast. A sun symbol, flanked by the zodiac signs for Aries, Gemini, Taurus, and Cancer, represents the months of March, April, May, and June, in which important historic events took place. A steamship with a Caduceus symbol as a mast represents the importance of trade to the country.

In a nation obsessed with soccer, it's no surprise that Ecuadorians are fanatical about the national team known as "La Tri" (short for La Tricolor, because they play in the colors of the national flag). The team has never won the regional Copa América cup, but support has grown immensely since they qualified for their first World Cup in 2002 and reached fever pitch when they got through to the 2014 World Cup in Brazil.

The most enduring and best-loved sporting hero is the long-distance race-walker and Olympic medal winner Jefferson Pérez.

More generally, if you ask ordinary Ecuadorians in the street what makes them proud they will point to the freshness, variety, and great taste of local dishes, the continuing tradition of local dress in the highlands, and the country's amazing ecological diversity, the snow-capped volcanoes of the Sierra, the steamy jungles of the Oriente, and the unique islands of the Galápagos archipelago and their connection through Charles Darwin with the Theory of Evolution.

Most of all, Ecuadorians will tell you that they are proud of the honesty, good humor, and friendliness of their fellow Ecuadorians.

ATTITUDES TO TIMEKEEPING

The mannered politeness, old-school reserve, and polished shoes of the more well-to-do inhabitants of Quito might create a sense that the Ecuadorian capital is akin to Britain in the 1940s, but it soon becomes clear that you're definitely in South America when it comes to issues of punctuality.

Ecuadorians will rarely arrive at the appointed hour and you are lucky if they are only fifteen or twenty minutes late. This is sometimes put down to traffic jams and the problems of parking in big cities like Quito and Guayaquil, but you are more likely to hear an excuse like: "Sorry, but nobody else is on time so we just get into the habit of arriving late." In some situations it is considered downright rude to be punctual, especially when arriving at somebody's house for dinner, as the hosts will probably not be ready.

For North American or Northern European visitors this flexible attitude to punctuality can lead to frustration—a feeling that many Ecuadorians share. On October 1, 2003, a campaign was launched to tackle this national epidemic of tardiness with a symbolic synchronizing of watches led by Jefferson Pérez, the country's first Olympic gold-medal winner. Suffice it to say that the campaign has had limited success. If you want to insist that something happens at an exact time you have to emphasize that the given time is *hora británica* ("British time").

RACE, CLASS, AND STATUS

Despite moves by the government to create a more inclusive society and reduce the large economic and social inequalities between rich and poor, Ecuador remains a country where people are still judged on where they were born, what they wear, how they speak, the color of their skin, and their last name. At the top of the pile are the rich elite of landowners, financiers, agro-exporters, and politicians who are considered Blancos (whites)—as much as a result of their social status as for the color of their skin. This small group makes up only around 6 percent of the population, but wields huge power and influence.

In Quito, for example, people still try to move to a desirable neighborhood in the north of the city as soon as they can afford to, as the rich and middle class have traditionally lived in the north of the city, and the working class and the poor in the south.

At the bottom of the social and economic ladder are the indigenous Ecuadorians of the Sierra and the Amazon region of Oriente, and the Afro–Ecuadorians of Esmeraldas and the Chota Valley. The working classes make up about 60 percent of the population, with about 25 percent of those living on or below the poverty line, compared to around 35 percent in 2007. Approximately 5 million Ecuadorians currently earn less than the minimum wage, which in 2021 was equivalent to US $400 a month. Overall, the economic situation of many became more precarious under the 2017–2021 Moreno government and was exacerbated by the Covid-19 pandemic that effectively shut down the informal economy of street traders.

Race remains a consequential factor in Ecuadorian society. Racist perceptions of indigenous people as lazy and slow are a legacy of Spanish rule, when the indigenous inhabitants of the Sierra were herded together on huge *haciendas* (estates, or plantations) and worked like serfs. Even after independence there was no change to this system—meticulously described in Jorge Icaza's 1934 novel *Huasipungo*—until the land reforms of the 1960s. Campaign groups have long fought for indigenous rights to ancestral lands, a greater appreciation of indigenous culture and traditions, and an end to racist attitudes. One of the main indigenous political groups, CONAIE (Confederation of Indigenous Nationalities of the Ecuadorian Amazon), rose in open revolt against the government in the 1990s, bringing down several governments. CONAIE also played a key role in widespread protests against fuel subsidies that the Moreno government tried to impose in 2019.

CONAIE estimates that more than a quarter of Ecuadorians belong to indigenous groups. Census figures often reflect lower figures as people choose to identify otherwise owing to negative attitudes to indigenous people.

ATTITUDES TOWARD FOREIGNERS

Ecuadorians are generally very welcoming to foreigners. In 2022 there were around ten thousand US expats living in Cuenca, Vilcabamba, Quito, Baños, and in towns along the coast between Salinas and Montañita, and the country has been hailed as an affordable and relatively hassle-free place to retire.

If there is any prejudice toward foreigners, it is directed mainly at the sizeable communities of Colombians, Peruvians, and Venezuelans in the country. Ecuador lost territory to Colombia in the nineteenth century and was swamped by large numbers of displaced refugees fleeing the conflict between the Colombian army and guerrilla groups prior to the peace deal with the FARC in 2016. Today, Colombian communities are largely located along the northern border around the town of Tulcan and in Santo Domingo de Los Tsáchilas, which some Ecuadorians have dubbed Santo Domingo de Los Colombianos. Colombians have a reputation for being involved in crime, but in general Ecuadorians and Colombians get on well. In the south there is a large community of Peruvians, who have a somewhat negative reputation for scamming, while Cubans, who came to Ecuador under cooperation agreements between former President Correa and the Cuban government, have gained a reputation for being loud and brash in conservative Quito where they have suffered some of the racial prejudice that darker-skinned Ecuadorians face. In Guayaquil they have found it easier to fit in.

The most recent wave of immigration occurred in 2017, when thousands of Venezuelans fled to Ecuador as a result of political repression and financial collapse at home. In 2022 there were more than four-hundred-thousand Venezuelans living in Ecuador and, while the majority were welcomed, there have been sporadic instances of friction over the diminishing availability of jobs in a challenging economic environment.

CHAPTER THREE

CUSTOMS & TRADITIONS

Following the conquest of the Inca Empire, Catholicism was imposed on the indigenous people by evangelizing Spanish priests, who incorporated local rituals and beliefs into church ceremonies to aid conversion of their new flocks. The result is a festival calendar that combines the movable feasts of the Church with indigenous customs and traditions, some of which date from before the Inca conquest. There is also celebration of important historical dates, such as the founding of the three main cities—a huge source of local pride—and the nineteenth-century battles that led to independence from Spain. Ancient beliefs and customs are preserved in the surviving myths and legends of Quechua-speaking highlanders and Amazonian tribes, in the healing rituals practiced by *curanderos* or *curanderas* (traditional healers), shamans, and *brujos* or *brujas* (witches), and in the production of traditional handicrafts.

FESTIVALS AND HOLIDAYS

There's a holiday, fiesta, or saint's day celebrated somewhere in Ecuador on nearly every day of the year, with some fiestas dragging on until the brass bands are too tired, or too drunk, to play any more. At some points of the year it can feel as if *días feriados* (public holidays) and *fiestas* (feast days or festivals) are running into each other to make one long holiday, especially in the capital, where Las Fiestas de Quito in November seem to last until New Year. March through June can also seem like an endless round of parties as movable feats like Semana Santa (Holy Week/Easter), Corpus Christi, and Carnaval converge into a blur of religious processions, marching bands, street parties, fireworks, and water bombs.

If you plan to travel to any of the major festivals or follow the crowds to the beach it is essential to book transport and accommodation well in advance, and expect bus and plane terminals to be very busy. Disruptions to the transport system at these times can leave you stranded in the more remote locations, so be prepared for delays. It is also typical for businesses, including government offices, banks, shops, and restaurants, to shut down completely on public holidays. When a public holiday falls on a Thursday or a Tuesday, many people will take an extra day off, known as a *puente* (bridge), to make a four-day weekend.

PUBLIC HOLIDAYS

January 1 Año Nuevo (New Year's Day)

February/March Carnaval (Carnival) Monday and Tuesday

March/April Semana Santa (Easter) and Viernes Santo (Good Friday)

May 1 Día del Trabajador (Labor Day)

May 24 Battle of Pichincha

July 24 Simón Bolívar's Birthday

August 10 Quito Independence Day

October Guayaquil Independence Day (First Friday after October 9)

November 2 Día de los Difuntos (Day of the Dead/All Souls' Day)

November 3 Cuenca Independence Day

December 25 Navidad (Christmas Day)

December 31 Año Viejo (New Year's Eve)

OTHER HOLIDAYS AND FESTIVALS

January 6 Día de los Reyes (Epiphany)

January 1-6 Diablada Pillareña, Pillaro (Devil dancers)

May, 2nd Sunday Día de la Madre (Mother's Day)

June, 3rd Sunday Día del Padre (Father's Day)

June 19-22 Inti Raymi, Cochasqui (Pre-conquest festival of the Sun held on Summer Solstice)

June 24 San Juan Bautista (St. John the Baptist)

June 29 San Pedro, San Pablo (St. Peter, St. Paul) in Otavalo and fishing communities, as these are the patron saints of fishermen

June, last week La Yumbada de Cotocollao coincides with San Juan Bautista and the Solstice with dancing by costumed Yumbos

July 26 National Sports Day

August 15 La Virgen del Cisne, Loja (Wooden statue of Virgin Mary taken in procession from El Cisne to Loja)

September Fiesta del Yamor, Otavalo (Maize harvest festival in honor of Inti, the Sun God)

September 23 Mama Negra de La Merced, Latacunga (First celebration of Mama Negra, with religious processions, led by a man on a horse with a blackened face and a black doll)

October 1 El Día del Pasillo Ecuatoriano

October 12 Día de la Interculturalidad y la Plurinacionalidad (Intercultural and Plurinational Day)

October 12 Fiesta de los Montubios (Rodeos and traditional dances, food in Guayas and Los Rios)

November Mama Negra Festival, Latacunga (A second celebration of Mama Negra, with brass bands, typical highland dress, masked dancers, parade)

November 3 Fiesta del Santo Negro, Canchimalero, Esmeraldas (Processions and dancing)

November 28–December 6 Las Fiestas de Quito (Parades, floats, dances, beauty pageants)

December 24 Nochebuena (Christmas Eve) (Nativity scenes, Christmas dinner, Misa del Gallo [Midnight Mass], children receive presents)

December 28 Día de Los Inocentes

El Año Viejo

On December 31 Ecuadorians bid farewell to El Año Viejo (the Old Year) and greet El Año Nuevo (the New Year) with a big party. All over Ecuador people make or buy papier-mâché figures called *monigotes*, which are

Papier-mâché *monigotes* are burnt to celebrate the New Year.

ritually burned in La Quema del Año Viejo (Burning the Old Year). Politicians, unpopular public figures, cartoon characters, and anybody who's been in the news are fair game. Some people write out a list of the bad things that have happened over the year so they can be burned with the *monigote*. It's quite a spectacle seeing hundreds of *monigotes* burning in the streets at midnight, and it's noisy, because many of them are filled with *camaretas* (fireworks).

In Quito and elsewhere, the festivities leading up to New Year's Eve include *viudas alegres* (merry widows). These are men dressed up to represent the Old Year's wife, who roam the streets drinking, dancing, flirting outrageously, and generally enjoying his demise.

At home people prepare a big meal, which is eaten late. Turkey is gaining ground as a festive food in the cities, and *cuy* (guinea pig) is still eaten in some parts of the Sierra. New Year's Eve parties are lively events, with dancing to festive music such as *cumbia*, *salsa*, *reggaeton*, and Latin pop. A New Year staple is "Yo No Olvido al Año Viejo" (I Don't Forget The Old Year), a song from the 1950s sung by Mexican crooner Tony Camargo.

Cábalas are superstitions aimed toward bringing good luck in the year to come. One popular custom is to wear red underwear to bring love, or yellow underwear to bring luck and money. Some people insist on wearing new clothes, to start the year looking good. To bring prosperity, some people will put $50 in their right shoe, or eat lentils. At the stroke of midnight the tradition is to eat twelve grapes with each of the twelve chimes counting down to the New Year, and wash them down with sparkling wine. In Quito they tune in to Radio Tarqui to hear the countdown. The last chime of midnight ends with deafening bangs as *monigotes* are consumed by flames in the streets and the parties start in earnest.

Carnaval

Falling on the weekend before Ash Wednesday, Carnaval is traditionally the last blast before the Lenten fast, so parades, parties, and music events are organized all over the country. Expect to get wet, as wherever you go there will be water balloons and surprise soakings.

Carnaval for many Ecuadorians means four or five days at the beach. The biggest organized event is in Ambato, where they hold the Fiesta de las Flores y las Frutas (Festival of Flowers and Fruit).

A masked reveler at Carnaval celebrations in Ambato.

Semana Santa

Celebrating the crucifixion and resurrection of Jesus
Christ, Semana Santa (Holy Week) starts with Domingo
de Ramos (Palm Sunday) and concludes with Domingo
de Resurrección (Easter Sunday). Popular ceremonies
include the *via crucis* (Stations of the Cross), when
devotees stage recreations of Christ's sufferings and
crucifixion. In Guayaquil on Viernes Santo (Good
Friday) there is a huge turnout of nearly half a million
people when the statue of the Cristo del Consuelo (Christ
the Consoler) is taken around the streets. In Quito the
procession for the statue of Jesus del Gran Poder (Jesus
of Great Power) from the Church of San Francisco
attracts thousands of penitents, including *cucuruchos*
("coneheads"), who dress in purple robes with cone-

Purple-robed *cucuruchos* mark Jesus' ressurection in Quito at the Semana Santa procession.

shaped hoods, and Veronicas, women dressed in purple with veils. There are also men dressed as Roman soldiers and people dragging heavy wooden crosses as an act of penitence and expression of faith.

Corpus Christi

Meaning "Body of Christ," Corpus Christi is celebrated on the ninth Thursday after Easter. In Cuenca, the holiday is extended for a week and is known as the El Septenario. This is a time to enjoy locally made sweets, cookies, and pastries. Massive towers of fireworks called *castillos* (castles) are the main attraction in the evenings. Typical tunes played at this time include the *Chola Cuencana* (Mestizo Girl of Cuenca), a *pasacalle* (passacaglia) composed by Rafael María Carpio Abad with words by the poet Ricardo Darquea Granda. In the market town of Pujili, located two hours from Quito in

Cotopaxi Province, indigenous dancers called "Danzantes del Sol" (Sun Dancers) pay homage to the Sun and the Moon, merging ancient Andean harvest rituals with Catholic imagery. Wearing masks and elaborate headdresses, they dance through the streets to the sound of Andean flutes and drums. The party continues

Fanesca

Not everybody takes part in the religious festivals during Semana Santa, but few Ecuadorians miss out on the opportunity to indulge in the filling festive soup known as *fanesca,* which is made from a base of *zambo* (gourd) and *zapallo* (pumpkin) with chunks of *bacalao* (salted cod cooked in milk). Holy as well as hearty, *fanesca* is supposed to be made with twelve types of grains or beans to represent the twelve apostles and decorated with slices of boiled egg, mini empanadas, white cheese, *palmitos* (palm hearts), *maní* (peanuts), and *plátano maduro frito* (fried ripe plantain).

Making *fanesca* is a tradition in many families who have their own recipes. There are even competitions in Quito and Cuenca, with prizes for the best *fanesca*. Following the Catholic tradition of abstaining from meat on Friday, this soup was traditionally eaten for lunch on Good Friday, but nowadays is eaten for the whole week leading up to it.

with brass bands playing dance music—starting with *sanjuanitos* and ending with *cumbia chichera*—and the crowds dancing and drinking.

Inti Raymi

Taita Inti (Father Sun) was one of the most important of the Inca Gods. Inti Raymi is the Sun Festival—held June 19–22 to coincide with the Summer Solstice and the maize harvest—giving thanks to the sun. The main celebration is held in Otavalo and the surrounding towns, with a smaller festival in the archeological complex of Cochasqui. Typical events include dancing in the Plaza de Ponchos, the drinking of *chicha* beer and *hervido* (cane alcohol and fruit), and ritual bathing in rivers and waterfalls, particularly the large waterfall in nearby Peguche. A central figure in the dances is Aya

Musicians at Inti Raymi celebrations in Cayambe, north Ecuador.

Uma, also known as El Diablo (the Devil), a mythical trickster character who wears a colorful two-faced mask topped by twelve snakes, representing the ancient wisdom of the indigenous people. Inti Raymi in its present form dates back to the 1970s, when indigenous Otavalans reclaimed the Inca name.

Paseo Del Chagra

Ecuador's mountain cowboys, known as *chagras*, are the focus of the Paseo Del Chagra (Parade of the Cowboys) held on July 23 in Machalila, just outside Quito. The festival dates back to 1877, when Cotopaxi erupted and the local priest went to the base of the volcano with a statue of Jesus. After the priest had held a mass the eruptions stopped, and the *chagras* made a triumphant procession back to town. Cowboys, cowgirls, and children ride horses around town in fluffy chaps called *zamorros,* before competing in rodeo events.

Fundación de Guayaquil

July 25, the anniversary of the day the Spanish conquistador Francisco de Orellana founded Santiago de Guayaquil in 1537, is the biggest party of the year in La Perla del Pacífico (Pearl of the Pacific), as Ecuador's largest city is known, The fiesta-loving locals combine it with the celebrations marking Independence hero Simón Bolívar's birthday on July 24.

Yamor Festival

This is the Chicha Beer Festival, held September 1–8, the second major festival in Otavalo. This festival dates from the 1970s, when local Quechua-speakers decided to revive an ancient tradition of marking the maize harvest in the days leading up to the September Equinox (known in Quechua as Coya Raymi). *Yamor* is the Quechua name for the *chicha* beer that was reserved for the aristocracy and the Sapa Inca himself. It is made with seven different types of maize and is sacred to the Inca deities Pachamama (Earth Mother), Taita Inti (Father Sun), and Sara Mama (the Maize Goddess). Bands play Andean songs on *rondador* pan pipes, flutes, violins, and guitars, there are parades and fireworks, and lots of soupy *chicha* beer. One of the highlights is the election of the Sara Ñusta (Princess of Maize), a beauty queen who must prove her knowledge of Quechua culture and traditions.

Mama Negra Festival

One of the most colorful festivals in Ecuador, the Mama Negra Festival in Latacunga, held on September 23–24, is a religious festival in honor of the Virgin of Las Mercedes but is also linked to the arrival of African slaves in the highlands. The strange cast of characters include El Rey Moro (Moorish king), El Ángel de la Estrella (Angel of the Star), and the Mama Negra, played by a local worthy who dresses as a woman, dons a black mask, carries a black baby doll, and follows the processions on horseback. Festival dishes include *champus,* a maize and fruit drink, and *chugchucaras*, a plate of pork rinds, deep fried pork, popcorn, potatoes, maize, and plantain.

Día de Los Difuntos

This is All Souls' Day, or the Day of the Dead, held
November 1–2. Families visit the cemeteries to tidy up the
graves of deceased relatives, celebrate their lives, and share
a picnic. Traditional Day of the Dead food includes *colada
morada,* a purple maize drink made with raspberries and
other fruit, and *guaguas de pan* ("bread babies"), sweet
rolls in the shape of dolls.

Independencia de Cuenca

Cuenca's biggest annual celebration, on November 3, marks
the city's independence from Spanish rule in 1820. The party
starts on November 1, and includes displays of fireworks,
marching bands, street processions, craft markets, and live
music events. The other big fiesta in Cuenca takes place on
April 12 and, rather ironically, commemorates the founding
of the city by the Spanish in 1557.

Virgen del Quinche

The small town of Quinche comes alive every November
21 as tens of thousands of pilgrims walk all or part of the
seven-hour trail from Cayambe to the shrine of the Virgin,
who is the patron of Ecuador. The first church built on this
spot dates from 1604, and the wooden statue of the Virgin
was carved by Don Diego de Robles, who also made the
Virgen del Cisne.

Las Fiestas de Quito

Quito is the party capital of Ecuador during the week of
fiestas, from November 28 to December 6, starting with a
beauty pageant to elect La Reina de Quito (Queen

of Quito), and continuing with live music events, floats, parades, parties in the parks, and colorfully painted buses called *chiva* buses. For many people the parties continue through to Christmas.

Navidad

Christmas is celebrated with masses and nativity plays in churches and schools on December 24 and 25. You will see *pesebres* (nativity scenes) everywhere, ranging from small wooden figures in people's homes to life-size manikins in public squares. It is traditional in many homes not to put *El Niño Jesus* (Baby Jesus) in the manger until Nochebuena (Christmas Eve).

In Cuenca, they hold an all-day procession on December 24 known as El Pase del Niño Viajero (The Procession of the Traveling Child), in which a statue of the infant Christ is paraded through the streets to the sound of brass bands and Andean flutes.

Masses leading up to December 24 are called *novenas*. Papa Noel (Father Christmas, or Santa Claus) is an increasing presence, and many Ecuadorian children now write letters to Father Christmas asking for gifts rather than El Niño Jesus as they did in the past. Presents are left under the Christmas tree or *pesebre* on Christmas Eve. Most families eat a late dinner, which may include turkey or chicken in city homes, or pork or *cuy* (guinea pig) in the villages, but will definitely involve a big sit-down meal with wine, whiskey, beer, or *chicha*.

The other major tradition is to go to church for the Misa del Gallo (Midnight Mass), which will be full

Holiday Calendar Reform

Columbus Canned

Celebrating Columbus Day on October 12, to mark the day in 1492 that Christopher Columbus is said to have arrived in the Americas, is no longer considered politically correct in Latin America, given the subsequent conquest, killing, conversion, and cruel treatment of indigenous Americans by the Spanish conquistadors. In Ecuador the day was renamed by decree in 2011 as Día de la Interculturalidad y la Plurinacionalidad (Intercultural and Plurinational Day). Former President Rafael Correa has said that it should be a day on which the country's rich ethnic diversity is recognized and all Ecuadorians, including indigenous groups and Afro–Ecuadorians, are united.

No Bull

Another major reform under former President Correa was the 2011 ban on bullfighting. It's not a total ban; tournaments where the bull is not killed are still allowed in some places, and bulls are still fought to the death in places where it is considered central to tradition.

to bursting in cities and villages alike, with *villancicos* (carols) sung to the accompaniment of the masses of fireworks set off in the streets. Día de Navidad

(Christmas Day) is a chance to open presents, visit family, and enjoy another big meal.

SUPERSTITIONS AND BELIEFS

Ecuador has a rich tradition of superstitions, myths, and ancient healing practices that we can only cover briefly here. From Europe comes a fear of black cats, and the idea that the number thirteen is unlucky—especially when the date is Martes 13 (Tuesday the 13th). Indigenous cultures carry on pre-Columbian beliefs that a spirit or soul resides in both animate and inanimate objects, so that trees, mountains, and lakes are considered living entities, and respect must be paid to them. It is typical to see people in the highlands sprinkling a few drops of alcohol on the floor for Pachamama, the Earth Mother, before drinking some themselves.

Highlanders believe that mountains and volcanoes are powerful entities because of their association with earthquakes, volcanic eruptions, thunder, lightning, and storms. The Inca temples and shrines on high mountains are no longer scenes of animal sacrifice or *chicha* ceremonies, but it is still held that you ignore these ancient spirits at your peril.

Andean villagers tie red cords or coral beads around their children's wrists to protect them against *mal de ojo* (the Evil Eye).

Traditional healers, known in Quechua as *yachacs,* are highly regarded in Ecuador and use a variety of techniques, including herbal medicines and ritual cleansing. The cleansing ceremonies to cure spiritual ailments like *mal aire* (bad air), or *espanto* (fright) involve incantations in Quechua, candles, blowing smoke on patients, beating them with herbs, and blowing alcohol on them. Some healers also draw out bad spirits with an egg that is rubbed all over the body, or with a live guinea pig that is slapped against the patient and then cut open to reveal where a physical problem may lie.

A shaman of the Amazonian Siona nation.

In big cities like Quito and Cuenca you can find herb stands in most big markets where ladies known as *limpiadoras* (cleansers) or *curanderas* perform many of these curing ceremonies with herbs and smoke and eggs.

In the jungle regions of Oriente, some groups are known for their past practice of shrinking the heads of warriors killed in battle so that they could keep the souls that reside in them. The Shuar tribe is famous for these shrunken head trophies (*tsantsas*), and also for the spiritual power of its shamans (*uwishins*) who use the hallucinogenic ayahuasca plant in their rituals.

Shamans from many different indigenous groups employ ayahuasca ("spirit vine") as a way of connecting with the spiritual world, and some now offer foreigners the opportunity to experience its powerful mind-altering effects in jungle retreats that mix New Age concepts with ancient shamanistic beliefs. The boom in Ayahuasca tourism has seen many retreats open that promise a cure to drug addiction, depression, and eating disorders but keep in mind that ayahuasca is a potent mind-altering psychoactive and should be approached with caution and through trusted practitioners.

MYTHS AND LEGENDS

In the villages around Chimborazo, the country's highest mountain at 20,564 feet (6,268 m), the locals say that if a pregnant woman is caught out in a storm she will give birth to an albino son of the volcano. They also say that Taita Chimborazo ("Father Chimborazo") is a jealous husband of the active volcano Mama Tungurahua ("Mother Throat of Fire"). When there are thunderstorms in the central valleys the locals say that Chimborazo and Tungurahua are having a domestic argument and throwing angry looks at each other. Chimborazo is also said to have smashed Carihuairazo and El Altar, two nearby volcanoes, in a love struggle over Tungurahua.

Similar tales are told in Otavalo about the two main volcanoes, Imbabura and Cotacachi, which are considered protectors of the people and the region. Cotacachi is sometimes called "Mama Cotacachi," or

"Maria Isabel Cotacachi," and there are many stories of her relationship with Taita Imbabura.

A stone in Peguche, known as "Achili Pachacamac," is considered sacred by Quechua speakers, and has been carved and decorated in recent times. Legend has it that Imbabura was fighting the nearby volcano of Mojanda for Cotacachi's affections and threw the stone at him, but it fell short as he had become weakened by his womanizing. Another story from Otavalo tells how an Inca prince and princess who were forbidden to marry threw themselves into the Mojanda volcano and resurfaced as the lakes Cariocha ("Man Lake") and Huarmicocha ("Woman Lake").

TRADITIONAL CRAFTS

The typical fedora hats worn by the highlanders are made in Iluman, a town famous for its *yachacs* (spiritual healers). In Cotacachi you can find all sorts of handmade leather goods. In Agato the local women still weave textiles on back-strap looms, and Zuleta is famous for the embroidered blouses worn by indigenous women in the highlands.

Tigua is famous for bright acrylic paintings of Andean village life, folk festivals, and ancient myths. They were originally painted on drums until the 1970s, when local man Julio Toaquisa decided to paint on canvas and a whole new style of folk art was born. There are several workshops to visit in Tigua, where you can see how the paintings are made and ask the artists about their inspiration.

The *tagua* nut, also called "vegetable ivory," was first carved into buttons in the nineteenth century by German settlers, who closely guarded the secret of what it was and where it came from. Small but attractive *tagua* figures are now carved in several places in Ecuador, especially in Sosote, in Manabí Province. A recent fad is to dye the nuts with bright colors, polish them until they shine like semi-precious stones, and set them in earrings, necklaces, and rings.

THE FAMOUS "PANAMA" HAT

A Panama hat is an essential purchase in Ecuador, whether you haggle over a $4 straw trilby sold at a Quito market or shell out $400 for a Superfino Montecristi at Homero Ortega's stylish shop in Quito. Found mainly in Manabí, the soft but very strong *paja de toquilla* (toquilla straw) used to make the hats was valued for its ability to shield against rain and was woven into headgear by indigenous people long before the Spanish arrived.

The traditional weaving of the toquilla straw hat is so important to Ecuador that in 2012 UNESCO added it to its list of the Intangible Cultural Heritage of Humanity.

The hat got its geographically confusing name when it became popular with workers on the Panama Canal in the nineteenth century and President Theodore Roosevelt was photographed wearing one on a visit to the canal in 1904. It has remained a classic summer essential ever since.

The name is such a strong brand identifier that Ecuadorians can't change it now. Signs stating "*Se vende Panama hats*" ("Panama hats for sale") appear even in the village of Montecristi, outside Manta, where the best *superfino* hats are woven by hand to exacting standards.

The big workshops are now in Cuenca, where the Museo del Sombrero de Paja Toquilla (Toquilla Straw Hat Museum) is a great place to see how the hats are made.

Light, hardwearing, and cool to wear, a hand-woven Panama hat will last a lifetime. The true test of quality is the tightness of the weave—so tight that it will hold water. Resist the temptation to try and pass the rolled-up hat through a wedding ring. Unless it's a good one, this will just ruin it.

CHAPTER FOUR

MAKING FRIENDS

Ecuadorians have a reputation for being polite and reserved, and in the highlands this can seem to stand in the way of making fast friends. However, despite an initial shyness toward foreigners, Ecuadorians are naturally friendly people who like nothing more than gathering together in groups to chat, tell jokes, eat, drink, and be merry. For a people who have known hardship and poverty in both past and present, Ecuadorians make the most of every opportunity to socialize.

THE LANGUAGE BARRIER

The first problem facing a foreigner who wants to make friends is the language barrier. The better your Spanish, the easier you will find it to meet Ecuadorians, because the majority of people, apart from the foreign-educated elite, or people who work in the tourism industry, know little or no English.

If you don't speak Spanish, or if you don't know a few phrases in Quechua to break the ice, you will be limited to very basic communication. If you're just in the country for a week to visit the Galápagos this won't be an issue. Equally, if you're in Guayaquil on a business trip, you should have no problems. If you are living or working in Ecuador, however, you will find it difficult to strike up spontaneous conversations and make friends. In this case it's a good idea to take a Spanish course, either for a few days, to give your confidence a boost, or for a few weeks, to go beyond the basics.

Quito and Cuenca are recognized as two of the top spots for studying Spanish in South America, because people in the cities of the Sierra have a high level of grammar, speak slowly and clearly, and the classes are good value for your money. Many schools offer homestay opportunities, where you lodge with a local family. Living, eating, and generally joining in the life of an Ecuadorian family is a quick way to pick up a lot of local vocabulary and a great way to make friends—many people keep in touch with their host families for years after their visit.

If you study some Spanish and use every opportunity to practice it on the Ecuadorians you meet, you'll soon see how hospitable people can be. Once they see you are making an effort, they will go out of their way to teach you new words and phrases, and make jokes you can understand so that you feel included in the conversation. Before you know it, your new Ecuadorian friends will be showing you how to dance *cumbia* and stuffing you with local snacks as they teach you how to read the menu.

THE FRIENDSHIP CIRCLE

Most Ecuadorians forge strong friendships at school as well as among cousins and other family members. By the time they reach adulthood they will generally have a tight group of friends that are like part of the family and will drop in unannounced for a visit and be invited to all the important parties and life events. Big families spend a lot of time together, and there are especially close bonds between brothers, sisters, and cousins. Friends outside the extended family will generally be school friends from primary school or university buddies, and an outer circle of work colleagues and other acquaintances, such as those who play in the same sports teams.

There isn't the need to find new friends in Ecuador as there is in North America or Europe, where nuclear families and moving out of the family home at a young age are the norm. Many Ecuadorians stay at home until they marry, and move back home again if they divorce, so their circle of friends can remain quite static.

This doesn't mean that foreigners won't make friends in Ecuador—quite the contrary! However, achieving the level of friendship where you are accepted into someone's inner circle of trusted friends is not something that happens overnight.

Unless you're in a relationship with an Ecuadorian and your partner invites you home to meet the family, it is rare to be invited to somebody's house. One reason for this is that extended families will often live under the same roof, which may make having guests difficult. There is also an issue of class and income. Most upper- and middle-class Ecuadorians have room for entertaining, and are used to doing so, but poorer people, although used to neighbors and close friends popping in unannounced, will rarely invite new friends around, preferring to meet them in bars or restaurants or at the park on a Sunday. The best opportunities to meet the family will be events like birthdays, christenings, and weddings, which are usually held outside the home.

FIRST CONTACT

Ecuadorians enjoy meeting foreigners, and given the chance they like to talk about their country and culture. The first contact is usually with the taxi driver taking you from the airport, the receptionist at your hotel, or the waiter serving you your first Pilsener beer. Use these opportunities to try out all the Spanish you can muster. Such conversations usually start with where you're from, how long you intend to stay in Ecuador, and where you intend to visit. The more positive noises you make about Ecuador and the Ecuadorians, the warmer the reception you'll get.

However, be wary of someone who comes up to you in the street and just starts a conversation for no reason. This might just be a simple hustler looking to make some cash out of a foreigner by taking you to a restaurant or store in return for a tip.

MEETING ECUADORIANS

Ecuadorian friends form close groups, so if you are invited to meet the other members of somebody's social circle it's a good sign—you have made a positive impression. You will be introduced to the group, and your own circle of friends will start to grow.

Be careful not to snub somebody by turning down an invitation to spend time with colleagues and new acquaintances, as you could give the impression you don't want to make friends and find that no further invitations come your way. Somebody who is perceived as an *aguafiestas* (killjoy) won't receive many more invitations to go out.

If you are working in Ecuador you will soon find that there is a strong social side to office life. Expect invitations to eat out for lunch or to grab a few drinks after work, and there'll be a regular parade of birthday cakes, a Secret Santa at Christmas, and even organized sporting events on the weekend, such as softball games or hikes in the Sierra. These are the first steps toward making friends, so take every opportunity that presents itself.

CONVERSATION STARTERS AND STOPPERS

Ecuadorians are happiest having light conversations that focus on positive impressions of their country. Typical questions will focus on your reasons for visiting Ecuador, where you have been, what foods you've tried, and a few questions about your family. Honest answers are appreciated, but steer clear of any criticism of the country, the people, the political situation, or the culture until you know people well enough to have a serious conversation. This is not because Ecuadorians don't criticize their country or don't like to debate the big issues of the day; they do—in fact, you'll find many Ecuadorians who are happy to list the failings of the president or the opposition, and lament the terrible traffic jams. But when a foreigner lists the country's failings it can come across as arrogant, especially given the country's love/hate relationship with the US over the years and the hard times many Ecuadorians experienced in the United States and Europe during the years of mass migration. This is an issue of pride and respect.

Avoid asking about the divide between the people of the Sierra and the Costa unless you know where everybody comes from in your group, as you could open old wounds and create an uncomfortable atmosphere.

People who are polite and keep conversations light and friendly will be seen as *simpático* (nice). People who try too hard to win an argument, or judge Ecuador too harshly, will be considered *antipático* (nasty).

INVITATIONS HOME

If you get an invitation to somebody's home then you know you've been accepted into the circle of trust. It's like saying you're one of the family, and it is a great honor.

The etiquette is quite simple: never arrive early or even at the stated time, as your hosts won't be expecting you to do so. As a rule of thumb, aim to arrive about twenty minutes late, and make a point of bringing something to drink. A bottle of good whiskey will always be appreciated, but if you know your hosts drink wine or beer then that's fine too. Ecuadorians are great consumers of sweet snacks, so pastries or fancy biscuits are another suitable gift. Dress casually, but on the sharp side. And expect to dance, even if the invitation is for dinner! Ecuadorians are passionate about music and after a few drinks you'll be invited to join in with a bouncy *cumbia* or swinging *salsa*. There's no pressure to impress—the idea is to have fun as a group.

CLUBS AND ASSOCIATIONS

Foreigners coming to Ecuador for any length of time should seek out some of the expatriate groups that meet up in the major cities, as they will help to ease your way into Ecuadorian society. You will find expat groups on Facebook for US and European citizens living in cities such as Quito, Guayaquil, and Cuenca, towns like Vilcabamba and Baños, and coastal resorts like Montañita and Salinas. Members of these groups will help you to meet Ecuadorians who speak English or like to hang out with foreigners, but it's best to avoid getting stuck in an expat bubble by learning Spanish and making Ecuadorian friends to practice with.

Ecuador's reputation as a top retirement destination has seen expat numbers rise dramatically in recent years, especially in Cuenca, which has attracted an estimated eight thousand US retirees, and the lively expat scene makes it easy to seek out your fellow countrymen and women. In towns like Baños and Montañita you only have to track down the microbreweries to find where the foreigners hang out, and Vilcabamba is so small you can't miss them.

In Quito, a good place to meet other foreigners and learn more about the country, the sights to see, and things to do is the South American Explorer's Clubhouse in the Mariscal district on Jorge Washington street, near the corner with Leonidas Plaza. Despite the name, the club is not just for avid explorers and mountain climbers: all are welcome. For a small membership fee you have access to the clubhouse and can sign up for the quiz nights and other events they organize.

Another members-only group is Internations, a global expatriate community with some four thousand members in Quito, Guayaquil, and Cuenca, that organizes monthly get-togethers.

DATING

Ecuadorians are very romantic—just listen to the lovelorn lyrics of the country's heartfelt songs in the *pasillo* genre. However, to have any success with a member of the opposite sex it is essential to learn the basic ground rules of the dating game, which can be very confusing for first-time visitors from the US and Western Europe.

While the rise of the dating apps like Tinder in the main cities and towns may have leveled the playing field a bit, by and large, men are expected to make the first move. For men from countries where it has become more usual for women to set the speed, taking the lead can be uncomfortable, but that's the way it works. Women tend to take a more subtle approach, dropping hints, while waiting for him to make the first move.

Whether you are a man or woman, don't expect to go Dutch if you want a second date. In all cases, men are expected to pick up the tab. If you are a man, suggesting splitting the bill at a restaurant with a date, or buying yourself a movie ticket and expecting her to do the same, is the kiss of death for any budding relationship. For women visitors, insisting on paying may well hurt an Ecuadorian man's feelings. Unless perhaps he's a *gringuero*—a man who intentionally goes after foreign women in bars and clubs.

A typical first date might be a meal at a restaurant, a visit to the movies, or just an afternoon stroll around a shopping mall. You may find when you have arranged a date with somebody that they turn up with a cousin or friend. Don't be put off. This is just a way of taking things slowly and getting to know you before taking any romantic plunge. And it might take several dates to get past holding hands. It's all part of the rather lengthy courting process that is usual in Ecuador.

Mixed Signals

When out in a bar or club, men should be careful not to misread signals. Just because a woman agrees to have a dance or a drink with you, it does not mean she agrees to anything else. Close dancing isn't seen as a promise of forthcoming romantic or sexual activity, as it might be in countries where people are not used to dancing together. Dancing is just a natural part of any social event in Ecuador, and all generations of an extended family or group of friends will happily dance all night together.

Ecuadorians are also very complimentary when chatting with friends. Men in particular can be very chivalrous, smiling and paying polite compliments (*piropos*) on a woman's appearance, and calling her *mi cielo* ("my heaven") or *mi corazón* ("my heart") just as a normal part of saying hello. By that token, a visiting woman also shouldn't either jump to conclusions or take offense if an Ecuadorian man spouts a few flowery phrases. It may well be that he does so to everybody.

You may also find that people ask very direct questions about your current romantic situation or past relationships, which should not be misconstrued as an indication of romantic interest.

For gay travelers, there are gay-friendly bars and clubs in Quito and Guayaquil, and a welcoming attitude in beach resorts like Montañita. Ecuador is still a traditional society in many ways, and public displays of affection between homosexual men or women in the street are not yet a typical sight. That said, things have come a long way in recent years (see page 57). There are now huge Día del Orgullo Gay (Gay Pride) parades in Quito and Guayaquil every July, and equality before the law is enshrined in the constitution.

In Quito there is a vibrant gay scene and making friends and filling your social calendar is easy. A good place to start is online. There are a number of Web sites listing gay-friendly clubs, and Facebook is home to a number of groups, including "Orgullo LGBTI Ecuador" with more than ten thousand members.

Ecuadorian Pick-up Lines

There was a time when Ecuadorian gentlemen would show their appreciation of a fair lady passing on the street by reciting a *piropo*, a line of romantic poetry. *Piropos* can sound quite cheesy to foreign ears. They usually revolve around stolen hearts, fallen angels, or stars in the sky. You still hear *piropos* like: "*Cada vez que pienso en ti, una estrella se apagará; te juro que pronto en el cielo no quedaría nada*" ("Every time I think about you a star stops shining; I swear that soon there'll be nothing left in the night sky"), or the classic "*Que alguien llame a la policía—me acaban de robar el corazón*" ("Call the police—somebody just stole my heart"). Not all *piropos* are sweet and innocent and there has even been a government campaign to put an end to crude *piropos* in the street, equating them with other forms of sexual harassment. If you hear somebody catcalling you, the best strategy is to do what Ecuadorian women do: ignore it completely and keep walking.

CHAPTER FIVE

THE ECUADORIANS AT HOME

Despite recent setbacks, Ecuador is on a trajectory of economic, social, and demographic transformation that is gradually bringing it up to date with the changes that have taken place in its neighbors Colombia and Peru. In a country where most of the population lived in rural areas in the central highlands, more or less since Inca times, rapid movement of people in recent decades has seen Ecuador become increasingly urbanized.

HOUSING

In the ultramodern sections of Quito and Guayaquil, the mega-rich occupy penthouses with extra rooms for live-in maids. City apartments overlook shiny new shopping malls, where shoppers purchase expensive imported goods, including many popular American brands. Quito is roughly divided into north and south; most of the city's poorer residents live in crowded

The colorful houses of Las Penas on Santa Anna hill, Guayaquil.

concrete housing blocks in the south while the more affluent middle class in the new part in the north.

After a multimillion-dollar regeneration project in the historic center of Quito—a UNESCO World Heritage Site—a process of gentrification has started that has seen the upper-middle classes moving back into the fine baroque houses that for now are home to multiple low-income families.

In Cuenca, middle- and working-class families live side by side in the well-preserved colonial buildings of the city center, but the pressures of a growing population have seen people with money move out to purpose-built condos and luxury apartments, many of them designed to meet the needs of the thousands of US retirees that have flocked to Cuenca.

A house in the Samborondon neighborhood of Guayaquil.

Many of the dusty towns you pass through in the interior look the same, with two-story cinder-block houses replacing the *bajareque* (wattle-and-daub) houses that you still see in highland villages. The only indications of wealth may be the fancy walls and manicured lawns around some of the houses.

One thing you find all over Ecuador, whether on the banks of wide jungle rivers, in the coastal lowlands, or in the brackish swamps of the Guayaquil slums, are houses built on stilts: the perfect antidote to rising waters and flash floods.

Elsewhere, in the jungles of Oriente, the Waorani continue to build thatched longhouses where several families can hang their hammocks around a central fire.

HOME HELP

You don't have to be rich to have home help in Ecuador. Wealthy and upper-middle-class families generally have one or more *empleadas domesticas* or *empleadas de hogar* (maids) living in the house to clean, cook, make beds, look after children, and do the shopping. Their flats and houses will include small bedrooms next to the laundry room that are specifically designed as maids' rooms. The word *sirvienta* (servant) will sometimes be heard in Ecuador to describe a live-in maid, although it is considered impolite and is best avoided. You will also hear an *empleada* described as *la muchacha* ("the girl"), even for maids in their forties or fifties, which can sound dismissive. To show respect, younger maids are generally addressed by their first names and older maids by their last names ("Señora Aparicio," for example).

The number of servants in a house is seen as an indication of status, but many families of lesser means among the middle and professional classes will also have some kind of home help, employing a cleaner for a few days a week rather than having a live-in maid. Even in poorer areas people will pay a neighbor to help with washing, cleaning, or childcare as needed.

FAMILY LIFE

Ecuadorians are very family-focused, especially outside the cities, where life is built around the home, and the extended family. Among the indigenous groups in

the Sierra and
Oriente, affiliation
to the tribe is also
very important,
and they continue
to practice ancient
traditions like the
minga (more on
that below).

Families
used to be big,
with eight or
ten children not
uncommon in
rural areas, but
now the average
family size in the
cities has fallen
significantly to
about 1.8 children

A young family in Quilotoa.

per urban couple. Children are doted on by parents and
grandparents, and have a godfather (*padrino*) and a
godmother (*madrina*)—often an aunt or uncle—who take
an active part in the child's upbringing. These *compadres*
("co-parents") are involved in key events in children's lives
beyond the baptism for which they are first chosen, and
will generally help with the costs and preparations for
the celebration of First Communion, Confirmation, and
quinceañera party.

Macho attitudes persist in Ecuador, and some men
believe that the number of children they father is an

indication of their manliness. This has led to a situation where men have children with multiple partners and then disappear, leaving the day-to-day upbringing of those children with the mothers and their families. This is particularly common in the poorer areas of big cities like Guayaquil and Quito.

Although assisted-living facilities exist, it is more usual for elderly relatives to stay with their families. Their pension contributes to the family finances and they may help out around the house by doing chores like cooking, cleaning, and looking after children, which frees parents to work.

Life can be a real struggle for poorer families, which generally have more mouths to feed, less disposable income, and a greater reliance on public healthcare, so every penny counts and the ability to pool resources from an extended family is crucial.

In the past, many young children had to work on farms and building sites to supplement the family income, and street kids would survive by shining shoes or offering to look after parked cars to raise extra cash for the family pot. Nowadays, the number of street kids in cities like Quito and Cuenca has been drastically reduced, although you will still see children working with their mothers as street vendors rather than going to school, and begging has not been entirely eradicated.

However, even the poorest family may invite a visitor in to have tea or coffee and a bite to eat. A popular saying is "*Donde comen dos comen tres*," which means, "Where there's food for two there's food for three."

THE MINGA: INDIGENOUS COMMUNAL SPIRIT LIVES ON

Many indigenous groups in Ecuador have maintained ancient traditions that help to foster strong bonds between individuals and families to the group. One such tradition is *minga*, which in Quechua means "a collective community endeavor." Just as many rainforest tribes live in a communal space and hunt, fish, and cook together, the indigenous groups of the Sierra work together when it comes to harvesting, planting, or building a house for a member of the community. This collective work is unpaid, but the beneficiary will provide food and drink (like *chicha* beer), and there might be a big party at the end. The *minga* is a Quechua tradition that has made its way into the mainstream of Ecuadorian society. A beach-cleaning campaign organized by an environmental NGO will be promoted as a *minga*, for example, or any collective community action to improve the conditions of local people, whether it's in the Sierra or one of Ecuador's big cities.

DAILY LIFE

On the Equator there are twelve hours of daylight and twelve of darkness, and the rhythms of life in the country still follow the rise and fall of the sun. Ecuadorians will generally start the day with a hot drink. Herbal teas are popular in the highlands, and coffee more popular in the coastal lowlands, but many indigenous people still just start the day with a cup of hot water, believed to clean the system. In the rainforests of Oriente, the local Quechua have their own morning kick-start in the form of *guayusa*, a plant with caffeine, vitamin, and mineral-rich leaves, boiled to make a tea.

For the middle and upper classes, US-style breakfast cereals have become popular, but for the average rural farmer or urban laborer a heavy meal of rice, potatoes, and *menestras* (beans or lentils) is still the way to start the day. For office workers, a rushed breakfast at home might be supplemented with an *empanada* (a filled bread or pastry snack) or a bag of crunchy, salted *tostado* (roasted maize) on the way to work. In the small towns of the Sierra, children waiting for the school bus may sip on hot *morocho* (a thick, creamy combination of cracked corn kernels blended with milk, cinnamon, sugar, and raisins).

Children will walk or take a bus to school, and start around 7:15 a.m., so early morning buses and trams are packed with commuters going to work and school children in uniform. Offices start work at about 7:30 or 8:00 a.m., and there is usually coffee available in large offices or a kettle or microwave for boiling water to make a herbal tea, or somebody comes around with a flask to sell watery black coffee in small cups.

Lunch is taken between 12:00 and 2:00 p.m. and is usually an hour long, although people stretch it to two hours when they can. With so many places offering a cheap fixed-price *almuerzo* (two-course lunch with a fruit juice or drink), most workers will have lunch out a few days a week. In rural areas, shops might close until 3:00 p.m. for a *siesta*—a short nap.

Offices close about 6:00 p.m., and some people in Quito and Guayaquil stop off at a mall to buy food in the supermarket before heading home, to avoid the rush-hour traffic. The evening meal is usually at home with the whole family seated at the table, and is taken at about 7:00 p.m. to 9.00 p.m.

Everyday Shopping

The growth of US-style shopping malls in all the major cities of Ecuador and the rise of national supermarket chains have luckily not replaced the habit of shopping at the country's marvelous markets. Indigenous craft markets, like the internationally famous Saturday market in the Plaza de Ponchos in Otavalo, draw in tourists and locals looking for good-quality clothes and textiles, but the heart of most towns is the food market. This is where the majority of Ecuadorians still shop for fresh fruit, vegetables, and meat. Neatly organized into sections selling different types of produce, Ecuadorian markets are also places where you can have a cheap *almuerzo* lunch, enjoy a fresh fruit juice, and even pick up some herbal medicine. In Baños market, for example, you can even visit a *curandera* for a healing whack on the back from a *cuy* (guinea pig) and then go outside and eat one of the little critters roasted on a stick (see Chapter 3 for more on Ecuador's traditional healers).

Everyday shopping is still done as it might be in a small town, in a *tienda de abarrotes* (grocery store), also sometimes called a *tiendita* ("little shop"); basically these are the mom-and-pop stores close to home that stock a little of everything. Every town and village in Ecuador will have at least one *tiendita*, a *licorería (liquor store), and a farmacía* (pharmacy), and larger towns will have a dedicated *panadería* (bakery). Street stands are also a very important aspect of the informal economy, selling everything from hot snacks to fresh produce, clothes, fashion accessories, and pirated CDs and DVDs of the latest music and movies.

Most people in the big towns will make a weekly trip to the local supermarket. There are several supermarket chains in Ecuador, including Aki, Supermaxi, and Mi Comisariato. They stock all the things you would find at home, although high import taxes make US imports expensive compared to locally produced alternatives.

Shiny shopping malls have sprung up all over Ecuador. The three-story Quicentro mall in Quito is enormous, with foreign clothing stores hawking goods at considerably higher prices than they do at home. Under one roof you can find a supermarket, bookstore, drugstore, and food court, with a McDonald's and other foreign and national fast food chains to choose from.

Quito, Guayaquil, Cuenca, and Salinas all have large, modern malls, many containing multiplex cinemas showing the latest movies. The prices may be too high for poorer Ecuadorians to afford, but the malls fill up at the weekends with window shoppers and moviegoers checking out how the other half lives.

RITES OF PASSAGE

For both rich and poor, there is a cycle of rites and rituals that follow the calendar of birthday celebrations, national holidays, and local festivities (see Chapter 3). Families also come together to celebrate the important milestones marked by the Catholic Church. The baptism of babies, where they receive their Christian name, is usually done soon after birth. First Communion, where the body and blood of Christ is consumed in the form of a consecrated wafer and a sip of wine, is typically undertaken in a group, with children aged from seven to twelve dressed in white, with white gloves and a white candle symbolizing purity. It follows a course of religious preparation and is an expression of faith in the Church. The final step is Confirmation, when at fifteen or sixteen years old a child expresses his or her commitment to becoming a full member of the Church.

Perhaps the biggest event for girls is the *Fiesta de Quince Años,* the party held when a girl turns fifteen (the *quinceañera),* which is seen as a rite of passage into womanhood and is rather like a wedding crossed with a debutante ball. An elaborate and expensive affair, it traditionally started with a mass in church (although this is being lost) and involves the girl dressing in a ballgown with a crown or tiara, and her friends and relatives in formal clothes. The typical protocol is for the girl to arrive at the party when the guests are all there, and for her father to change her flat shoe for a *zapatilla* (shoe with a high heel) to symbolize her new status as a woman. She then dances a waltz with her father, and maybe another dance with her boyfriend, and there is a toast before the partying starts in earnest. For the rich elite, *quinceañera* presents can be a car, an apartment, a trip abroad, even plastic surgery. Many poorer families can't afford the expense of a big party, but will definitely have a celebration that includes a dress and a cake.

Weddings

There are few festive occasions in Ecuador as joyous or costly as a wedding. For the elite a wedding involves a number of parties and related events, including a civil wedding, which is normally held at home, and a lavish church wedding and reception. The dress code is rented tuxedos for men and ballgowns for women. Once again, the *padrinos* (godparents) are involved alongside the best man and chief bridesmaid and the reception will include uniformed waiters offering appetizers before a toast, a first waltz with the father of the bride, the dance of the happy couple, and then dinner, followed by music and dancing to a live band or DJ until the early hours.

Civil ceremonies take place before a justice of the peace either in the civil register offices or at home. Those who can afford to have a civil wedding at home decorate their house or apartment, invite their friends, and have a party after saying their vows and signing the book.

The rate of marriage in Ecuador has been in decline in recent years as couples choose to wait longer before tying the knot or decide to live together without a formal marriage. In the past, women often got married under the age of 23, particularly in rural areas. Today, an average age of 23–25 is the norm for women, while for men it is 25–29.

A wedding in the Church of Our Lady of Guápulo, Quito.

Although Ecuador is a Catholic country, divorce has been legal since 1909 and is not a complicated process. As children are given both paternal and maternal surnames, there is no real stigma nowadays in being the offspring of an unmarried couple. Rates of divorce have been steadily rising in recent decades; for example, between 2006 and 2016 rates rose by nearly 90 percent.

CHAPTER SIX

TIME OUT

Life revolves around food in a big way in Ecuador. The profusion of street snacks, the hawkers on the buses selling sweets and savories, the lines outside cafés and restaurants at lunchtimes, and bustling markets brimming with fresh produce all confirm the national obsession with good food.

As we have seen, Ecuadorians also adore family life, and take every opportunity to get together in their free time and enjoy a meal, celebrate a birthday, or throw a big party.

A busy calendar of public holidays and Catholic festivals and feast days means the average Ecuadorian has more family time than the two-week summer vacation enjoyed by most Americans and Northern Europeans. An Andean wedding can go on all day and all night. A village *fiesta* can last a week and bankrupt the person known as the *prioste* who is given the privilege (and cost) of organizing it.

On weekends, people head for the parks, which are always full of children's parties and picnics, or set out for the beach or the mountains to make the most of a *puente* (long weekend). In Quito, roads are closed off on Sundays to create a cycle route that brings whole families out on their bikes. Parks have jogging trails, sit-up benches, and dip bars for an outdoor workout. Popular sports played on weekends and in the evenings include soccer, another national obsession, and Ecuavoley, a local version of volleyball which has its own rules.

For the less energetically minded, shopping malls are great places for city folks to spend the day people-watching and snacking on fast food at the food court, while up in the highlands, the colorful markets attract locals who come to socialize as much as they do to shop.

Music is an integral part of Ecuadorian cultural life, from the haunting sounds of the indigenous Andean panpipes to the deafening bash of brass bands at village *fiestas* or the electronic *cumbia* music called *chicha* that fuels parties in mountain villages and city parks alike. Latin pop, *salsa*, and reggaeton are hugely popular in clubs in the cities, while surf resorts up and down the coast prefer a laid-back reggae vibe.

FOOD AND DRINK

The difference between the highlands and the coast also extends to food, with pork, potatoes, and maize being staples in the Sierra, while fish, seafood, and plantains dominate on the coast, with peanut sauces being popular in the coastal region of Manabí. Popular dishes from the highlands include *hornado* (roast pork), which is sold from roadside vendors or market stands that display whole roasted pigs. Typically it's served with *llapingachos* (mashed potato and cheese patties cooked on a griddle). *Fritada* is fried pork and is also served with *llapingachos*, fried *yuca* and *plátano* (plantain), or *mote* (homily).

Just in case you haven't had enough pork, try some *chicharron* (pork rinds). *Seco de chivo* (goat stew) is typically served with rice and plantains. *Menestras* are lentils or beans served with *carne* (beef) and rice. *Empanadas* are turnover pastries filled with cheese, beef, or chicken that make good snacks. *Patacones* are unripe plantains fried, squashed flat, and fried again to produce thick chips. *Bolon de verde*, a popular breakfast option on the coast, consists of deep-fried balls of mashed plantain stuffed with cheese or *chicharrón* that are traditionally served with fried eggs and a black coffee.

Ecuadorians like their food spicy and make *salsa de aji* (hot sauce) of varying degrees of fierceness from local Serrano chili peppers. The hottest *aji* is made with red chilis mixed with salt, lemon juice, oil, onions, and cilantro (coriander). In some places they add the juice of the *tomate de arbol* (tree tomato) and *chochos* (lupini beans).

Soups

Ecuador is renowned for its hearty soups, which are a key part of any *almuerzo* (set lunch). Visitors are often amazed at the side dishes they are served with: slices of *aguacate* (avocado), *canguil* (popcorn), *tostado* (toasted corn nuts), *arroz* (rice), *patacones* (thick plantain chips), *chifles* (thin slices of fried plantain), and even *chicharron* (pork rinds). The most famous soup is *locro*, a thick potato soup containing chunks of cheese. *Yaguar locro* is potato soup with blood sausage. *Encebollado de atún* is a fish stew made with tuna, onions, tomatoes, and cassava, that is prized as a hangover cure and eaten for breakfast in many places. *Caldos* are more like broth, and include *caldo de patas* (cow heel soup) and *caldo de gallina* (chicken soup). *Guatita* is a hangover cure made from cow tripe. The soup that makes some visitors nervous is *caldo de nervio,* or *caldo de tronquito,* a stew made from chopped bull penis, that is sometimes sold as "natural Viagra" and is more popular than you might think.

Chochos—Approach With Caution

There is one staple part of the Andean diet that you should always approach with caution. Lupini beans (*Lupinus mutabilis*) are small, white beans known as *chochos* in Ecuador. High in protein and other nutrients, they are extremely popular, sold on the streets from buckets by indigenous vendors, and added to salads and sauces in upscale eateries. However, they are bitter and slightly toxic in their natural state, and the beans have to be soaked and boiled and soaked again for three days before they can be eaten. While *chochos* bought in shops and served at restaurants are generally reliable, some street traders soak their beans in the river, and this can lead to stomach upsets.

Fish and Seafood

Along the coast and in the main cities, Ecuadorians enjoy a large choice of *pescado* (fish) such as *corvina* (sea bass), *pargo* (red snapper), *cherno* (grouper), and *picudo* (swordfish), usually served with *patacones* (thick plantain chips), rice, and a simple salad. In Esmeraldas the emblematic dish is a delicious *encocado de pescado* (fish cooked in coconut).

Ceviche is a way of marinating fresh fish or seafood with lemon juice and *aji* (peppers) that originates in the Andes. Shrimp must be boiled before being marinated, but fish and seafood are effectively "cooked" in the citric acid of the lime. Before the Spanish brought limes from Europe, historians say *ceviches* may have been marinated in *chicha* beer. You can find *ceviche* made with *camarones* (shrimp), *calamares,* (squid), *cangrejo* (crab), *concha negra* (black clams), *pulpo* (octopus), *langostinos* (jumbo shrimp), *erizos* (sea urchins), or a combination, called *mixta*. Ecuadorian *ceviches* tend to be sweeter than Peruvian *ceviches* because in Ecuador they add fresh tomato, freshly squeezed orange juice, and finely chopped red onion to the marinade to balance the citric bite of the limes. Ecuadorians also love to mix tomato ketchup and yellow hot dog mustard into their *ceviches*.

Vegetarians and Vegans

Vegetarians have plenty of fruits, soups, vegetables, pizzas, pastas, and pastries to choose from in Ecuador, but should always be careful when ordering food. *Sin carne* only means "without beef," not "without meat," and there may be little understanding of "*Soy vegetarian*"

("I'm a vegetarian") in the highlands or jungle. For vegans, many *ceviche* places will prepare a *palmito* (palm heart) or *chocho* (lupini bean) *ceviche*.

CRAZY FOR CUY

Fluffy pet or tasty snack? Ecuadorians in highland villages laugh when foreigners are squeamish about snacking on *cuy*, the local name for a guinea pig (*Cavia porcellus*). Guinea pigs have been eaten in the Andes for some five thousand years and provided a valuable source of protein when the only other domesticated animals were llamas and alpacas. They breed at a fast rate and are highly nutritious. Typically kept in the kitchen, they run free, feeding on food scraps. They are a popular food at festivals and weddings, and grace the Christmas table in many a highland home. *Curanderos* (healers) also use them in traditional medicine.

Before being roasted whole on the barbecue they are stretched out flat, their big buck teeth making them look quite strange. The skin is basted with fat to give it a golden color and a crispy texture, and the delicious meat tastes like a cross between chicken and rabbit. Restaurants in Quito, Cuenca, and Baños all serve *cuy*, but they are not cheap, and might cost as much as $20 for a whole *cuy* with potatoes. If you just

Waitresses serve up grilled *cuy* and fried potato balls.

want a small portion to say you've tried one, ask for a leg—"*una pierna, por favor*"—otherwise you might be honored with the *cabeza* (head) and have to nibble around those choppers.

When the Spanish conquistadors arrived in the country they called these little critters *conejillos de india* ("little Indian rabbits") and brought them back home, starting a craze for keeping them as pets. The English monarch Elizabeth I famously kept guinea pigs.

Amazing Maize

The variety of ways that Ecuadorians eat maize (corn, or Indian corn) is quite astonishing. It is toasted, boiled, popped, ground to make a dough, fermented to produce a mildly alcoholic beer, or boiled up in a hot milky drink. And if you think popcorn is something you only eat at the movies or while stretched out on a couch, in Ecuador you can enjoy it sprinkled on soups or as a side dish at lunch. Recent archeological discoveries show that popcorn—known by the Quechua name *canguil*—was a key staple of early Andean civilizations as far back as four thousand years ago.

Another ancient use of maize that's enjoyed today is *maíz tostado*, or toasted maize kernels, served as a side dish with soups and *ceviche*. These are often referred to in English as corn nuts, because the kernels are crunchy and salty, like peanuts. *Chulpi* is like a *tostado*, but sweet. Boiled corn on the cob, called *choclo*, is a standard ingredient of soup, adding a touch of sweetness. A great favorite in the highlands is *mote* (hominy), a variety of maize with large white kernels that are peeled by soaking in slaked lime (calcium hydroxide) and boiled before being served alone or as an accompaniment to pork dishes like *hornado* or *fritada*. A breakfast dish from Cuenca, called *mote pillo*, consists of *mote* fried with onions, eggs, milk, and fresh cilantro or parsley. *Humitas* are made from ground maize mixed with different ingredients, particularly cheese, and then wrapped in a corn husk and steamed. They are popular as a breakfast dish or as an afternoon snack in the highlands. Variations include the bigger *tamales* (doughballs stuffed with chicken or fish and boiled in a banana leaf), which are eaten at Christmas.

Evidence of boiling and fermenting maize to make a weak beer known as *chicha* has been found in the ancient Valdivia culture of the coast, and probably goes back much earlier. When the Sapa Inca Atahualpa had his first meeting with the emissaries of Pizarro he served the Spanish conquistadors a special *chicha* made by the *acclas*, or Virgins of the Sun. *Chicha* beer is still the accepted payment for communal work in the highlands known as *minga* (see page 109). It is such an important element of Andean civilization that there are several festivals in honor of *chicha*. The Festivales de La Jora in Cotacachi and the Yamor Festival in Otavalo celebrate the maize harvest and the days leading up to the solar equinox on September 22. The *chicha* beer served in Yamor is made from seven varieties of maize, including black, yellow, white, *chulpi*, *mote*, and *jora*. *Chicha morada*, or *colada morada*, is an unfermented, non-alcoholic version of *chicha* beer made from purple maize and fruits like *piña* (pineapple), *frutilla* (strawberry), and *mora* (blackberry). Families take *colada morada* and *guaguas de pan* (bread babies) to cemeteries as a gift for their ancestors during the Day of the Dead celebrations on November 2.

A sweet, creamy drink called *morocho* is made from boiling milk and maize flour with cinnamon and *panela* (unrefined sugar).

Desserts

Ecuadorians have a sweet tooth and enjoy cakes, pastries, and desserts like *dulce de leche,* also known as *manjar de leche,* which is made from sweetened condensed milk that is heated until it turns into a runny caramel. Other favorites are *dulce de higos con queso* (figs cooked in a syrup made from boiled cane sugar served on soft white cheese), *quesillo* (crème caramel), *torta de zapallo* (pumpkin pie), and *quimbolitos* (sweet corn cakes with raisins). Fresh fruit prepared in a fruit salad is also typical, as are mousses made from *maracuyá* (passion fruit) and *guanábana* (soursop). *Helado de Paila* is a type of handmade fruit sorbet or ice cream that is made with sugar and egg whites in large copper pots.

EATING OUT

Ecuadorians love to eat out. In the main cities there is a wide range of restaurants to choose from, as well as fast food outlets, hole-in-the-wall eateries called *huecas* or *dolarazos,* food stalls in markets, and street vendors. On the beaches of the coast there are mobile *caretillas* (bicycle-mounted food stalls) that sell *ceviches* and other traditional dishes. You even have people getting on the bus to sell sweets and savory snacks to hungry passengers.

At the top end of the scale are fine-dining restaurants that offer gourmet twists on traditional dishes—see for example restaurants like Zazu, Quitu, the Casa Gangotena, and Theatrum Restaurante and Wine Bar in Quito. In the middle are a profusion of Italian and other restaurants selling a variety of international dishes. Fast-food outlets like McDonald's, KFC, Domino's Pizza, and American Deli are considered middle class, and are located in the food courts of the biggest shopping malls, like the Quicentro in Quito, the Mall del Rio in Cuenca, and the massive Mall del Sol in Guayaquil. More recently

TIPPING

Giving a tip for good service is not compulsory in Ecuador. Locals rarely add any extra to a restaurant bill at an upscale eatery, which will already include an added 10 percent service charge and 12 percent tax. At informal places, where you pay no tax, there is no need to tip. Keep in mind that most staff in restaurants and hotels are low earners, so if you feel the waiter, maid, or bellhop went out of their way to help you, feel free to pass on your appreciation in the form of a dollar or two.

When taking a guided tour at a jungle lodge or in the Galápagos, the usual rate for tipping guides is anything from $5–$10 a day; you can pay more or less depending on the service you receive. Don't forget something for the driver or boat crew.

If you are driving, there's no need to tip gas attendants unless they wash the windows and check the tires.

the home delivery market has taken off with the arrival of food ordering apps like Uber Eats and Glovo.

The best value meals are found in places offering an *almuerzo* (a set lunch). This generally includes a juice, a hearty soup, a main course of meat, chicken, or fish served with potatoes or rice, or *menestras* (lentils) or *plátano* (plantain), and a dessert. Costing anything from $1.50 to $3, *almuerzos* are served in *huecas* or at covered markets. For many workers, this is the main meal of the day, and you find lines outside the popular places at lunchtime. Set dinners, known as *meriendas*, are more expensive and not so popular, because less affluent Ecuadorians are more likely to have a meal at home with the family.

Chinese restaurants called *Chifas* are found all over the country. The two staples at *Chifas* are *chaulafan* (fried rice with chicken, shrimp, or both) and *tallarines* (noodles).

A very Ecuadorian snack sold from food carts is *salchipapas*, consisting of a portion of fries and a frankfurter sausage drizzled in ketchup and served in a plastic bag. It doesn't sound particularly appetizing but tastes good after a night on the town.

Drinkers in Cuenca, Baños, Guayaquil, and other places can sober up with a late-night *shawarma*, a pita stuffed with spit-roast meat, and falafel.

On Sundays and special occasions like Father's Day it's typical to visit a *cevichería* for a plate of shrimp, fish, or seafood marinated in lemon juice and tomato. *Asaderos* specialize in rotisserie chicken; *parilladas* in barbecued meat, chicken and *chorizo* (pork sausages); and *marisquerías* in seafood.

Drinks

One benefit of being on the equator and having so many microclimates in one country is the abundance of exotic *jugos* (fruit juices) available, from *piña* (pineapple) and *frutilla* (strawberry), to *mora* (blackberry), *maracuyá* (passionfruit), and *sandía* (watermelon). Some local fruits are seldom found outside the region, like the sharp but delicious *tomate de árbol* (tree tomato) and the creamy *chirimoya* (custard apple). In sugar-cane areas you can get *guarapo,* juice squeezed straight from the sugar cane. Juices are sold in restaurants, cafés, markets, and street stands.

Most Ecuadorians will drink water from the tap in the bigger cities where water is treated, but on the whole, visitors should opt for bottled, filtered, or boiled water, or carry a travel bottle with an inbuilt filter to eliminate bacteria and parasites. Even treated water in cities can be affected by old piping systems, and so the cautious and those susceptible to stomach ailments should stick to bottled water. In restaurants, water is generally filtered (*agua purificada*), but if in doubt, ask.

Ecuador produces excellent coffee beans, but the best-quality coffee was always exported, leaving Nescafé and similar brands of cheap instant coffee for local consumption. Luckily the situation has improved, and in most places, you can now get good, freshly made coffee. The main coffeeshop chain is Juan Valdez from Colombia, but there are plenty of small Ecuadorian cafés serving coffee made from premium local beans.

Teas are very popular, and many Ecuadorians start the day with an infusion of *manzanilla* (chamomile), take oregano tea for an upset stomach, and prepare a refreshing cold drink called *horchata* from a cure-all mix of herbs. A jungle tea called *guayusa,* prepared for years by the Kichwa people of the Amazon, has high caffeine levels and is used in traditional healing. It is also added to homemade cane alcohol in some regions to produce a cocktail with an added kick.

Alcoholic Drinks

Ecuadorians are primarily beer drinkers and will always find an excuse to enjoy an ice-cold *cerveza* (beer). The leading brand is Pilsener, a light, refreshing, good-value lager beer with the inviting slogan: *Ecuatorianamente refrescante* (Equatorially refreshing). It is closely followed by Club Premium. Both brands are owned by the multinational beer giant SABMiller. A more recent entry to the market is the sweeter Brazilian beer Brahma, owned by the Belgian-Brazilian multinational Anheuser-Busch InBev. Foreign beers such as Heineken and Guinness are stocked in some supermarkets and available at international hotel chains, but these are more expensive, owing to the high taxes on imported goods.

In Quito, a couple of microbreweries serve more

adventurous beer options, such as Belgian ales and German-style dark beers. In Baños the La Cascada Brewery produces ales, porters, and stouts for the Stray Dog Brewpub, and in Montañita you can sit in front of the surf sipping a pale ale, stout, or porter, thanks to the Montañita Brewing Company, owned by a local US expat.

Andean *chicha* beer is made from fermented maize and sugar (see above) and is worth a try. Down in the Amazonas region the *chicha* is made with cassava that's been chewed and spat out so that the saliva can aid the fermentation process and may upset delicate stomachs.

Foreign spirits are expensive, due to high taxes aimed at supporting local brands, and whiskey, while popular, is not for all. Most Ecuadorians stick to the excellent local rum, like Ron Canuto, or less sophisticated *aguardiente* ("firewater"), a white sugar cane alcohol. Popular *aguardiente* brands are Zhumir, Cristal, and Manabí. *Canelazo* is a hot mix of *aguardiente,* sugar, lemon, and cinnamon that keeps the cold at bay on a chilly Andean evening.

Traditional countryside moonshine made from distilling *guarapo* (sugar cane juice) in an *alambique* (copper still) is known as *puntas* and plays a big part in many local fiestas, although it should be avoided by those unused to its throat-burning alcohol content.

Wine is taxed at a lower rate than spirits but is still expensive compared to the US or Europe. High-end restaurants offer a good selection of Chilean and Argentine wines and most supermarkets stock a range of wines to suit most tastes and budgets.

MISKE MEZCAL

Ecuadorians down gallons of distilled sugar cane *aguardiente* every year, but sugar cane is not native to the Americas and so the main contender for Ecuador's national drink has to be miske, a distillation of agave sap that is an Andean version of Mexico's mezcal, but whose flavor is entirely unique. The sweet-tasting sap gathered from the heart of the agave is called *chaguar mishqui* or *tzawar mishke* and is traditionally fermented into a form of beer called *guarango* that is drunk at highland festivals. When the Spanish conquest brought the copper still to the Americas and *guarango* was distilled, the fiery spirit miske was born. Produced in artisan distilleries in the agave-growing areas of the highlands, miske is confusingly labeled as mishqui, mishky, and even tequila in some places. As its popularity increases at home and mezcal lovers abroad discover miske's unique flavor profile, indigenous

producers are finding new markets for their small batch productions. There's even a miske museum, the Casa Agave, where you can taste the best of the country's agave spirits.

National soccer legend Antonio Valencia.

SPORTS

Ecuadorians are soccer mad. The national team is affectionately known as "La Tri" (short for La Tricolor, after the country's three-banded flag), and whenever a big international match is on, especially against rivals Colombia and Peru, you'll find crowds cheering them on at cafés and bars. For a small country, Ecuador has a decent record in international matches over the last twenty years, qualifying for the World Cup in 2002 and making it to the final sixteen in 2006 in Germany before being knocked out by England. The 2014 World Cup in Brazil saw them beat some of the best teams in South

133

America, although they didn't make it past the group stage. Ecuadorians are hopeful of their team's chances at the 2022 World Cup in Qatar after not qualifying in 2018.

In May 2007 it looked as if Ecuador would be unable to host World Cup qualifying matches at its main Atahualpa Stadium in Quito after FIFA introduced a ban on international matches at more than 8,200 feet (2,500 meters), citing medical fears for the players and the alleged unfair advantage it gave the high-altitude host nations. A concerted campaign by Ecuador, Bolivia, Peru, and Colombia led to the ban being dropped the subsequent year.

La Tri has benefited greatly from players gaining experience in Latin America and Europe. One of Ecuador's biggest stars was Antonio Valencia, who signed a multimillion-dollar contract in 2009 with English Premier League leaders Manchester United and played for the club for ten years, making 325 Premier League appearances, a record for a South American player. Valencia, who retired in 2021, was born in the Amazon oil town of Lago Agrio, and is an example of how soccer can dramatically change the lives of Ecuadorians from humble backgrounds with a natural talent for the beautiful game.

Ecuavoley

While soccer is a national passion, Ecuador's national sport has to be *ecuavoley*, a unique version of volleyball that pits three against three, is more relaxed on ball-holding than the European six-on-six or Brazilian two-on-two game, and has a higher net at 9.2 feet (2.8 meters).

CHOTA VALLEY: A SOCCER FACTORY

Ask any Ecuadorian where the best soccer players come from and the answer will invariably be the Chota Valley in the northern provinces of Imbabura and Carchi, where a small but significant community of Afro–Ecuadorians lives, breathes, and sleeps soccer. The inhabitants of these dusty, valley-bottom towns are the second-largest black community in Ecuador after Esmeraldas. Descended from slaves brought from Africa in colonial times, they were organized in *huasipungos,* like the local indigenous groups, and put to work on sugar plantations. Today, Chotanos still maintain African drum music and dancing traditions, like *la bomba* and the bottle dance (where women dance with a bottle balanced on their heads). But it's their skill at soccer that most characterizes the local people, and it's a source of great pride.

Chota Valley players who have had success in foreign leagues—like Ulises de la Cruz and Agustin Delgado, who both played for English clubs— have been instrumental in turning round years of government neglect here by building schools, medical facilities, and, of course, soccer academies. Success in soccer has provided a way out of the local poverty trap for gifted young players and has acted as a partial antidote to the widespread racism and marginalization of black communities that was endemic in Ecuador until recent years.

The players are called the *servidor* (server), *ponedor* or *colocador* (setter), and *volador* (flyer), and the game is played with a football on hard concrete courts. The referee is called *el arbitro* and teams play two sets of fifteen points each. The first *ecuavoley* neighborhood tourneys were set up in 1943 in Quito, where the first championship was played in 1958, and it has now spread to every corner of the country. Tournaments are taken very seriously, but in street games it's not unusual to see players taking sips of beer as a part of the fun, and betting on the sidelines to add to the excitement.

Cycling

To encourage cycling, Quito's main North–South arteries are closed on Sundays from 8:00 a.m. to 2:00 p.m. to create a 19 mile (30 km) cycling route that runs through

The Locomotive, Richard Carapaz.

sites including Parque La Carolina, La Mariscal and Parque El Ejido, Parque La Alameda and the old town. Bikes can be rented along the route if you want a workout but be aware that the altitude can leave you breathless until you acclimatize. Mountain biking is popular in the highlands, with many trails around Baños and other mountain towns. For adrenalin junkies there's a white-knuckle ride down the slopes of Cotopaxi.

Local rider Richard Carapaz, or the "La Locomotora" (The Locomotive), as he is affectionately known, made history in 2019 as the first Ecuadorian to win the Giro d'Italia. In 2021 he was elevated to national hero when he won gold in the cycling road race at the Tokyo Olympics.

Surfing

Ecuador's year-round good weather and high waves at Pacific beaches like Montañita have led to a growing surf scene. The 2013 ISA World Masters Surfing Championship was held in Montañita, which along with the southern coastal town of Salinas, also hosted the World Surf League's men and women's qualifying competitions in 2022. Manta and Punta Carnero are also popular surfing spots and you can even surf in San Cristóbal in the Galápagos Islands. The main surf season is January through May, but you'll find surfers hanging out in Montañita all year round, giving the place a unique and laidback vibe.

Hiking

Trekking and climbing are year-round pastimes, but make sure to take a few days to acclimatize to the altitude

137

The crater lake of Quilotoa volcano in the Andes.

before you set out and always check on recent seismic
activity if planning an ascent of volcanoes like Sangay or
Tungurahua. The tricky two-day ascent of Cotopaxi is not
for novices as it takes you 19,347 feet (5,897 meters) above
sea level and involves climbing a glacier, but anybody
reasonably fit can take on the three-day circuit through
beautiful Andean valleys to the Quilotoa crater lake.
Road runners might prefer the Guayaquil Marathon held
on the first Sunday of October around the city's major
landmarks. Held since 2005, it was initially dominated
by Colombians, but Ecuadorian runners are now taking
away the top prizes.

Sporting Legend

Ecuador's first Olympic medal winner is Jefferson Pérez, who won the 20 km Walk at the 1996 Atlanta Olympics when he was just 22, becoming the youngest person ever to win the event. To the great delight of his fans in Ecuador, he picked up a silver medal twelve years later at the 2008 Beijing Olympics. Born in humble circumstances in the Cuenca neighborhood of El Vecino, Perez sealed his international status and place in the record books after winning his third successive 20 km Walk World Championship in Osaka in 2007. He is seen as a role model for Ecuador's young athletes, and a national hero. The date of his 1996 Olympic victory, July 26, is now celebrated as Ecuador's National Sports Day. Pérez was the first to congratulate the Ecuadorian team at the 2021 Tokyo Olympics when they set a new national record by winning two golds and one silver medal in cycling and weightlifting.

CINEMA

A boom in the Ecuadorian film industry following the creation of the CNCine (Consejo Nacional de Cinematografia) in 2006 has seen film production jump from a movie every three years in the mid-1990s to ten or eleven films a year since 2012. Directors to look out for are Cuenca-born Sebastian Cordero, whose 2011 film *Pescador* ("Fisherman") tells the tale of a fisherman whose unremarkable life takes a dramatic turn when he finds cocaine washed up on the beach. *Sin Otoño, Sin Primavera* ("No Autumn, No Spring"), a tale of teen rebellion and confusion that throbs along to the sound of the Guayaquil rock scene, was directed by Iván Mora Manzano. *A Tus Espaldas* ("Behind Your Back"), directed by Tito Jara, explores indigenous identity, class barriers, and racism in Quito.

Leading the new wave is director Tania Hermida whose 2006 movie *Qué Tan Lejos* ("How Much Farther?") won several international awards, as did her 2011 follow-up *En Nombre de la Hija* ("In the Name of the Girl"). Javier Andrade, whose film "*Mejor No Hablar*" ("Best Not to Speak") was Ecuador's entry to the 2014 Oscar's, scored another international achievement when his spooky psychological drama "*Lo Invisible*" was selected for the Toronto International Film Festival in 2021.

Ecuador is also doing well on Netflix—Jorge Ulloa's 2019 frenetic youth comedy *Dedicado a Mi Ex* ("Dedicated to My Ex") proved extremely popular across Latin America. One of the most unusual films to come out of Ecuador in recent years is director Paúl Venegas' 2019 movie *Vacío* ("Emptiness"), a tale of illegal Chinese immigrants seeking their dreams in Guayaquil's China Town. There are modern *multicines* (multiplexes) in large shopping malls in all the big cities, but Ecuador only has some 250 cinemas in total. English-language movies are shown either *doblado* (dubbed into Spanish) or *con subtitulos* (subtitled).

ART

Art is everywhere in Ecuador, from the pre-Columbian gold and ceramics on display in museums to the colorful textiles and tapestries woven today by the descendants of those first Ecuadorians. The collision of Spanish Catholic culture with traditional Andean and Inca culture led to a process of *mestizaje* (mixing or fusion) that went beyond a mixing of races.

Colonial-era churches were built on the ruins of Inca temples as a way of showing who was in charge, but the profusion of gold leaf in places of worship echoes ancient Inca practices.

So many churches, monasteries, and convents were built in the first years of the conquest that Spanish artisans couldn't keep up with the demand, and the Escuela Quiteña (Quito School) was founded at the Church of San Francisco. Here, indigenous painters and carvers were trained to produce Catholic religious art for the Royal Audience of Quito until they surpassed their Spanish masters. For more than three hundred years, artists and craftsmen in Quito supplied artworks to the capital cities of Latin America and even exported to Europe, such was their fame.

The exquisite baroque and rococo masterpieces of art and architecture found in Quito and Cuenca are among the best-preserved in Latin America, and it's easy to see why they were declared UNESCO World Heritage Sites. A good example of the syncretism and cultural blending that defines the Quito School is the *Last Supper* in the Cathedral Church painted by Manuel Samaniego y Jaramillo (1767–1824). Instead of a Passover lamb in front of Jesus there's a roast *cuy* (guinea pig) and the disciples are drinking *chicha* (fermented corn beer) and eating *humitas* (corn bread). Another star of the Quito School was the *mestizo* (mixed-race) artist Bernardo de Legarda (1700–73), who created the sculpture of *The Virgin of the Apocalypse* for the Church of San Francisco in 1734. Better known as *The Virgin of Quito*, or *The Dancing Virgin*, the small wooden sculpture shows a winged Virgin Mary trampling on a dragon and beating it with a silver chain, that was inspired by a passage in the Book of Revelation. A 150-foot (46-meter) replica now stands atop the Panecillo, a hill that was sacred to the sun in Inca times. Designed by the Spanish artist Agustín de la Herrán Matorras, the iconic statue is made of seven thousand pieces of aluminum and was completed in 1976.

Following the Wars of Independence, artists like Antonio Salas (1780–1860) focused on portraiture of national heroes and patriotic scenes as the new nation sought to define itself. So-called *costumbrista* paintings by Joaquín Pinto (1842–1906) depicting local customs and everyday life added to the nation-building drive. Modernism came to Ecuador in the 1930s with a strong influence from the Mexican muralists and a determination to depict the plight of Ecuador's downtrodden and exploited indigenous population. Artists like Camilo Egas (1889–1962) and Eduardo Kingman (1913–98) led this move toward socially engaged *indigenismo* (indigenism), which was echoed in the writing of authors like Jorge Icaza and his most famous novel *Huasipungo*. Ecuador's greatest modern artist, Oswaldo Guayasamín (1919–99), was also inspired by the Mexican muralists and fired by a rage against the pain and suffering endured by the poor and marginalized sectors of Ecuadorian society. The brilliance of Guayasamín lies in his combination of elements from Expressionism, Cubism, and pre-Columbian art to create a signature style that is instantly recognizable.

Ecuador's contemporary art scene includes an exciting variety of styles and mediums. Standout names include Pablo Cardoso, Jorge Velarde, and José Bastidas, while artists such as Daniel Adum Gilbert and Belen Bike adorn city walls with graffiti-inspired street murals.

THE ART OF SUFFERING

Few painters are as instantly recognizable as Oswaldo Guayasamín. The twisted hands, screaming mouths, and haunted, emaciated faces of his mature work seem to take elements from Picasso's famous anti-war painting *Guernica* and the powerful depictions of saintly suffering captured by the Quito School painters and fuse them into a moving portrayal of indigenous suffering in Ecuador and beyond.

Guayasamín was a lifelong follower of left-wing causes and is famed for his portraits of the Cuban revolutionary leader Fidel Castro. In 1988, a mural he painted in Ecuador's Congress angered the US government because it showed a dark figure in a Nazi helmet with "CIA" written on it. Ironically, Guayasamín's first taste of international fame stems from the purchase of five of his works in 1942 by Nelson Rockefeller, which led to his first exhibitions in the US. His final masterpiece is the *Capilla del Hombre* ("Chapel of Man"), a museum built to showcase giant murals of his work alongside his collections of pre-Columbian artifacts and artworks from the Quito School. It was finished in 2002, three years after his death. A quote on the wall of the chapel sums up the artist's commitment to social causes: "I cried because I didn't have shoes until I saw a kid who didn't have feet."

MUSIC

Ecuador's diverse cultures are reflected in the many different genres of music you will hear as you travel around the country. Pan-Latin American rhythms and dances like *salsa*, *merengue*, Latin pop, and reggaeton are also popular, with an extra dose of reggae at surf spots along the coast. The term *música nacional* ("national music") covers everything from pre-Inca melodies played on indigenous panpipes to Afro–Ecuadorian drum dancing, and a genre of sad songs known as *pasillos* made internationally famous by the celebrated Julio Jaramillo

(1935-78), whose birthday on October 1 is now celebrated as El Día del Pasillo Ecuatoriano (Day of the Ecuadorian Pasillo).

Highland festivals and *fiestas* swing to the beat of *sanjuanitos*, a genre of Andean dance music named after the San Juan Bautista festival on June 24 but which dates from Inca times, and the Inti Raymi celebrations for the Sun God which took place around the same time (see Chapter 3). *Sanjuanitos* are played on *bandolín* (mandolin), *charango* (a small ukulele made from an armadillo shell with two sets of five strings), guitar, and *bombo* drums. Bamboo flutes like the *quena*, *pingullo*, and the *rondador* (panpipes) give the music a haunting, melancholic edge. Once heard mainly around Otavalo and Imbabura Province, *sanjuanitos* are now popular at parties and *fiestas* across the highlands and in Quito. Electric guitar, bass, and Yamaha organ are sometimes added to the mix, and it's not unusual to find a village brass band banging out *sanjuanitos* at a local *fiesta* or wedding reception.

Afro–Ecuadorian music can be divided into two genres: *marimba* music in Esmeraldas, and *bomba* in Chota. The *marimba* is a percussion instrument with wooden bars that are struck with mallets. Native to West Africa, it is played like a xylophone and typically accompanies a large *bomba* drum, a *cununo*, which is like a tall bongo drum, and a *guasa*, a bamboo tube filled with seeds that is shaken. In Esmeraldas they dance the *bambuco* and *caderona* with African call-and-response vocals. Afro–Ecuadorian music in Chota has absorbed elements from indigenous Andean music to produce a dance called *bomba* that is played on *bombo* drums and guitars. Banda Mocho is a Chota music institution, keeping alive the extraordinary tradition of playing vegetables as if they were brass band instruments and leaves as if they were clarinets or trumpets. The *bomba* is such a staple of Ecuadorian culture that *cumbia* bands will play it at parties.

One feature of traveling by bus in Ecuador is the TV at the front, playing music videos featuring girl bands in knee-length boots with names like Grupo Deseo, Doble Sentido, and Las Diablitas. These groups sing along to tinny *cumbia* and *salsa* tracks played on a Yamaha organ and a metal scraper. This type of *cumbia,* known as *chicha* or *cumbia chichera,* is hugely popular and incorporates elements from Andean music to give it a local flavor.

LITERATURE

Ecuador's most renowned writer is the novelist, playwright, and cultural ambassador Jorge Icaza (1906–78), who achieved international fame with his 1934 novel *Huasipungo* (published in English translation as *The Villagers*). A masterpiece of Latin American fiction, the book tells the tragic tale of the injustices and exploitation doled out to the indigenous population of the highlands by rich and ruthless *patronos* (landowners) in conjunction with a compliant and corrupt Catholic Church and greedy foreign capitalists. Icaza employs Quichua words and phrases in the book to capture the authentic voice of the villagers. A bestseller when it first came out, the book went through three revisions by the author until the definitive version of 1960. It has been translated into eleven languages, including Russian and Chinese, and sold millions of copies. No other Ecuadorian writers have enjoyed such success, and the local publishing scene is hampered by a small readership.

Contemporary author Gabriela Aleman bucked the trend with her 2007 novel *Poso Wells*. A tale of criminals, call girls, and corrupt politicians set in the seedy underbelly of Guayaquil, it was republished in Spain in 2012 with illustrations by Spanish graphic artist Tebo. Other notable contemporary authors include Guayaquil-born Mauro Javier Cardenas, whose 2016 debut novel, *The Revolutionaries Try Again,* tells the story of three childhood friends who contemplate a revolution as Abdalá "El Loco" Bucaram's madcap election campaign exposes the buffoonery, brutality, and greed of Ecuador's political class.

Another contemporary talent is Mónica Ojeda, whose fantasy horror novel *Mandíbula* was published in English as *Jawbone* in 2022.

Other notable writers and poets from Ecuador's past who have helped to shape the country's sense of identity are Juan León Mera (1832–94), who wrote the national anthem, and liberal essayist and writer Juan Montalvo (1832–89), whose literary attack on dictatorship helped to bring down Gabriel García Moreno. After García Moreno was hacked and shot to death by a mob in Quito on August 6, 1875, Montalvo wrote: "It is My Pen that Killed Him!"

CHAPTER SEVEN

TRAVEL, HEALTH, & SAFETY

Ecuador is relatively small and travel within the country is cheaper than in the US or Europe, easy to organize, and relatively safe. The locals love to point out that you could breakfast at a pristine beach on the Pacific coast, lunch by a snow-covered volcano in the high Andes, and dine in a jungle camp surrounded by rainforest and rare birds.

As elsewhere in the tropics, healthcare is an important consideration. Prevention is better than cure, so ensure you get all the necessary inoculations before you travel, and take sensible precautions over food, drink, and exposure to the sun. Travel insurance is essential, and should cover everything you do during your stay, including adventure sports if you plan to climb a volcano, scuba dive, or go whitewater rafting.

The cities of Quito and Guayaquil have their fair share of pickpockets and scam artists ready to prey on unwary visitors, so it is important to take care of yourself and your belongings, particularly when sightseeing or traveling at night. There are also some security hotspots along the Colombian border that should be avoided, and these are outlined below.

BY AIR

With airports in most major cities and towns, and short flying times, traveling around Ecuador by plane is a good, safe option if you have limited time. The two major hubs for international flights are Quito and Guayaquil, and the flight between them takes an hour.

Quito's Mariscal Sucre International Airport in Tababela is Ecuador's busiest airport. About 22 miles (37 km) by road from the city center, it opened in 2013 with the goal of boosting the number of flights coming into the capital and expanding the number of long-distance connections with airports in the US, Europe, and South America. It is roughly a forty minute taxi ride to downtown Quito from the airport.

The two airports in the Galápagos at Baltra and San Cristobal are served by flights from Guayaquil (an hour and a half) and Quito via Guayaquil (three hours). Rainforest tours in the northern Oriente start in Coca, a forty minute flight from Quito.

BY TRAIN

The glory days of Ecuador's 1067 mm-gauge railroad network—when locomotives linked the towns and villages of the Andes and carriages were packed with

A train descends the Devil's Nose (Nariz del Diablo), in Alausi, Chimborazo.

woolly llamas, squeaking guinea pigs, and indigenous farmers taking their merchandise to market—ended in the mid-1990s when landslides and poor maintenance saw most of the lines close. For a while, the only option for travelers looking for an Andean rail experience in Ecuador was an *autoferro* (a diesel bus on rails) that ran along the picturesque Avenue of the Volcanoes.

Everything changed in 2008 when the country's rail infrastructure was officially declared a "Symbolical Historical Patrimony of the Ecuadorian State" and the government began to revamp the rail network as a tourist attraction. A government-owned rail company called Ferrocarriles del Ecuador Empresa Publica (FEEP) was created in 2010 and new track was laid, old stations revamped, new carriages and steam locomotives brought into service, and the historic

Trans Andean line between Quito and Guayaquil was reopened. A four-day Tren Crucero (Cruise Train) tour—inspired by other great train journeys around the world—took wealthy tourists and steam train enthusiasts to stations turned into mini museums of local culture, with craft displays and shows of local dancing, as well as excursions to visit cocoa plantations and historic haciendas.

The jewel in the crown of Ecuador's mountain rail network is the trip from Alausí to Sibambe that features 7.5 miles (12 km) of switchbacks, perpendicular drops, and gives a real sense of the cutting-edge engineering (literally in some places) that was employed to get trains 1,640 feet (500 m) down a steep mountain wall known as the Nariz del Diablo (Devil's Nose). Started in 1901 and completed in 1908, the US engineers employed a series of switchbacks, so the train has to shunt forward and then shunt backward as it zigzags its way down the mountain. The work was so dangerous that an estimated 2,000 Jamaican and Puerto Rican workers died during the construction of the Nariz del Diablo section, earning it the nickname as "The most difficult railway in the world."

After running the rail network at a loss for many years, the government decided to liquidate FEEP in 2020 and all lines were closed. The most popular routes along the Avenue of Volcanoes and the Nariz del Diablo are expected to reopen in private hands as working railroad lines, or as hiking trails, given the spectacular nature of the scenery.

Quito Metro

Designed to ease the capital city's traffic chaos, an ambitious $2 billion project to create a fifteen station metro line running through the city from north to south has been under construction since 2012. Plagued by delays and funding shortfalls, the city metro system is planned for open in late 2022, though further delays are expected. When operational it will run from El Labrador in the north to Quitumbe in the south and have an end-to-end journey time of thirty-four minutes. It is expected to transport some 350,000 passengers a day.

ON THE ROAD

An extensive program of infrastructure projects and road improvements, combined with a greater emphasis on enforcing traffic laws, has cut road journey times and made traveling safer. High mountain roads, poor signage, landslides, and mist and fog at altitude, however, still cause bus accidents, especially at night. In Quito, the number of cars and taxis on the roads lead to gridlock at peak hours, but a bus and trolleybus service with dedicated lanes and fixed bus stops helps to reduce travel times. Elsewhere, in the country, rules are more lax, and buses will still stop at any point along the road where passengers want to get off. For public transportation timetables you can use the Moovit App, while downloadable countrywide maps for offline use can be found on the MAPS.ME app.

Taxis

With stiff competition for fares keeping journey prices low, taxis are a great way to travel in Ecuadorian cities, especially after dark, or when traveling to places where security is an issue. Taxis are easily identified on the streets, as they are painted yellow and should have orange license plates, unlike private cars, which have white plates. They also have a four-digit registration number on the front doors. Never take a ride in an unlicensed taxi—known as *piratas* ("pirates")—as you could end up being the victim of a so-called "express kidnapping" (see page 167).

A typical ride within most towns and cities costs between $2 and $5, but taxi drivers are known for inflating prices when they see a foreigner coming, so always negotiate a price before you climb into the cab. At the main airports it's hard to get a good deal unless you leave the airport and hail a cab on the street, but considering the fare between Quito's Mariscal Sucre International Airport and the center of town is 22 miles (37 km) and the fare is only about $30, it's easier and safer to get an official airport taxi.

In Quito, Cuenca, and Guayaquil taxis are supposed to use meters, but only in Quito are the regulations strongly enforced. Even in Quito, if you're traveling early in the morning or late at night taxis will try to find an excuse for not using the meter, and will generally double daytime prices. Always clarify the situation with the meter before you start your journey.

EasyTaxi is the main ride-hailing app in Ecuador, though Uber has been expanding its presence and offers Uber Pass discounts on taxi rides and Uber Eats.

City Buses

Quito, Guayaquil, and Cuenca all have efficient and cheap bus services, although gridlock at peak times can make progress slow, even with dedicated bus lanes, and pickpockets are a problem. In Quito, bus routes run along the north to south axis linking the popular hotel and bar district of Mariscal with the historic old town, charging about 25 cents a journey. Make sure you have coins to pay with.

Alternatively, for the same price, with concessions for senior citizens, you can use one of the city's alternative bus systems: *El Trole, Ecovia,* and *Metrobus.* *El Trole* is a very efficient trolleybus system that runs for about 11 miles (18 km) from the north of the city to the main intercity bus terminal at Quitumbe in the south. With dedicated lanes linking the main stations along the north-south line, it is the fastest way to beat the traffic, and transports some quarter of a million passengers every day. Buses usually display their destination (and sometimes stops along the route) on the front, but always ask the driver if he stops at your destination before you get on.

Intercity Buses

Each city and large town has its own *terminal terrestre,* with bus companies serving destinations all over the country. There are frequent departures on hundreds of buses of different levels of comfort, from chicken buses linking remote mountain towns to shiny, air-conditioned intercity buses with reclining seats and on-board entertainment. Bus terminals are generally clean and modern, with food vendors and bathroom facilities, but always take care of your belongings, as they may attract pickpockets and bag snatchers.

For short trips you can jump on a basic *buseta* (small bus with limited leg room and local stops), or you can buy tickets in advance for *buses de lujo* (luxury buses), which are more comfortable for long trips and will show a DVD en route (although expect some dire US shoot-em-up or inappropriate erotic thriller).

In smaller towns and villages there may be no bus station, and people will simply gather at a spot on the side of the road and wait for a bus to pass through. Ask locals where to stand and when the last bus comes through, as some buses will stop running in the afternoon and the only alternative could be a *camioneta* (see below) or an overnight stay.

For safety reasons it is better to travel in the daytime, as accidents and hold-ups are more likely to occur at night. Given the size of the country, journey times are relatively short to most destinations and prices tend to be no more than $1 an hour. A bus from Quito to Cuenca will take anything from eight to twelve hours and cost around $10 to $12. From Quito to Baños is about three and a half hours and costs about $3.50 to $4. Whatever the quality of bus you get, expect itinerant hawkers to get on and launch into an elaborate sales pitch that far outstrips the value of the sweets or Korean ginseng capsules or nail clippers they are trying to sell you.

Colorful Local Transport

In the beach resorts and fishing villages of the coast, you'll find fairly "homemade" cycle taxis (*bici-taxis*) and motorbike taxis (*moto-taxis*) that are cheaper even than yellow cabs and can take up to four passengers. In rural areas where bus services are limited or nonexistent, *camionetas* (pickup trucks) operate as an informal bus or taxi service between towns and villages. They have no set schedules or stops and leave when full. Alternatively, if you are in a rush you can pay a set rate and leave when you like. Always try to ask locals how much they pay

Yellow and black *moto-taxis* wait for passengers in the small coastal town of Puerto Lopez.

before you agree to a price with the driver. If not, you might be paying for the families that get in the back of the truck as you pull out of town. The most colorful way to travel is on one of the brightly decorated country and coastal buses known as *chivas* ("goats"), so named because they were brought in to tackle steep mountain roads. They have bench seats that slat straight across the width of the bus with open doors at each end and are also sometimes called *escaleras* ("ladders") because of the ladders on the back of the bus that allow passengers to put their baggage, assorted merchandise, and livestock on the roof. The roof is also a great escape for passengers looking for respite from the crush of people squashed into the knee-numbing space between the benches. Increasingly common are *rancheras,* which are bench-seat *chivas* mounted on a truck base instead of a bus base. In Quito and other places, there are city tours on *chivas* that can get very lively at night as the buses travel from venue to venue with live music, singing, dancing, and local hooch to get the party started on board.

DRIVING

Rental Cars

With gas prices so cheap and so many places to visit within a relatively short driving distance of Quito, Guayaquil, and Cuenca, it might be worth renting a car from one of the many international or local car rental firms that operate at most airports. However, with driving conditions so different from those at home and taxis also being very reasonably priced, you may find it worth paying a local driver to take you out on day trips. This can avoid any problems if you have an accident as Ecuadorian road rules are strict and drivers can be held in custody if there's any argument over who is responsible for a crash. If you do decide to rent a car you will need to be at least twenty-five years of age, have a valid driver's license (from your own country or an international license), and pay with a credit card. Read the contract carefully and factor in the extra taxes charged and insurance costs. Always check the brakes, seatbelts, and tires, and make sure there is a working car-jack (*gato*) and spare tire (*llanta de repuesto*). Note any dents with the rental agency before taking the car and take photos of anything you might have difficulty explaining afterwards. Highways and city roads improved greatly under former President Correa who invested in major infrastructure work, but country roads can still be hit and miss, and poor weather conditions can make driving difficult. If you do rent a car, you can use Waze to navigate the roads.

Rules of the Road
Ecuadorians drive on the right, as they do in the US, but the driving experience is quite different and the rules of the road only began to be strictly enforced in recent years. Drivers have to be both aggressive, to make progress in traffic, and defensive, as other

drivers swerve around and cut in front of each
other, overtake on both sides, and honk their horns
impatiently. The situation is not helped in the main
cities, where a horde of yellow taxis and motorbikes
leads to gridlock at peak times (see below on Pico
y Placa).

Drivers and front-seat passengers must wear
seat belts, and if you don't comply with this and are
stopped by the traffic police, you'll be fined. There is a
speed limit of 31 mph (50 kmph) in cities and 59 mph
(90 kmph) on main roads, and police charge drivers
with breaking the speed limit. Slightly over the speed
limit and you get a fine and six points on your license;
significantly over the limit and you get a hefty fine,
ten points on your license, and three days in jail.

Breathalyzers (*alcoholímetros*) are a fairly recent
introduction and are increasingly being employed
at night to cut down on driving under the influence.
These state-of-the-art machines have a camera to
take a photograph of the person being tested and are
linked to a central computer that instantly provides a
list of all previous infractions and license details. They
have even been installed at the country's twenty-two
main bus stations in an effort to reduce the number of
bus-related accidents.

Parking infractions can also lead to stiff fines and
impounding of your vehicle, so always look out for a
sign with a capital "E" with a diagonal slash through
it, which stands for "*No Estacionar*" (No Parking).
In Quito they have a system called *Zona Azul* (Blue
Zone) with boxes marked in blue on the road. The

idea is that you pay an attendant about forty cents an hour for a maximum stay of two hours, but very often they are not easy to find. Make sure you do find one, though, as vehicles that don't pay and display a ticket sold by the attendant are clamped and then towed to the Metropolitan Police pound.

PICO Y PLACA

The Pico y Placa ("Peak Hour and License Plate") is a program that aims to reduce traffic congestion, encourage the use of public transport, and cut air pollution in the center of Quito during the weekday peak hours of 7:00–9:30 a.m. and 4:00–7:30 p.m. Basically, the last digit of a vehicle's license plate determines which day of the week it can be used. Only buses, taxis, and cars owned by seniors (people over sixty-five) and the disabled are exempt. The traffic police take this seriously, and to ignore it can prove costly. A first offense carries a $122 fine and the car is impounded for twenty-four hours, for a second offense it's $189 and the car is impounded for three days, and for a third offense it's $366 and the car is held for five days. A similar system was imposed for several months in the city of Guayaquil to reduce traffic during the Covid-19 pandemic.

HEALTH

Before You Travel

Ensure that you have adequate travel and health insurance to cover treatment in case of accident or illness. The best policies cover you for emergency medical transport, evacuation, and repatriation. This is particularly useful if you plan to travel to the Galápagos Islands, where medical services are limited.

Have the required immunizations in good time before your departure. A tetanus-diphtheria booster shot is recommended if you haven't had one in the last ten years. Typhoid, Hepatitis A, and Hepatitis B are also recommended.

Pack long pants, and shirts with long sleeves, and bug repellent, because in the rainforest the mosquitoes come out to bite as the sun is setting. Also pack sunhats and sunscreen. Traveler's diarrhea is common, so pack Lomotil or a similar product, which will help when traveling on flights or long bus journeys. Rehydration salts will also help you to feel better.

On Arrival

Quito is the highest capital city in the world, and visitors who fly in feel some effects of altitude sickness, although generally these are only minor symptoms such as shortness of breath, dizziness, or drowsiness. The secret is to drink plenty of liquids and take things easy while the body acclimatizes. You should also avoid excessive alcohol intake, and swap coffee for one of the excellent herbal teas they drink up in the highlands, such as *manzanilla* (chamomile). In some hotels they will even provide a cup of hot coca tea, a traditional Andean remedy for *soroche* (altitude sickness). If you experience more serious symptoms, such as headaches, nausea, or confusion, it is important to monitor the situation, but rehydration and rest will generally be enough to get you through the first day. If symptoms persist and get worse after two or three days, you should see a doctor. There are some medications that are prescribed for altitude sickness, such as acetazolamide, but the simple act of descending to a lower altitude is the most effective response.

Take Precautions

Ecuador is a hot, tropical country with year-round sunshine, and as such visitors should take basic precautions when spending time in the sun. Sunburn is not just a problem at the beach but in the mountains where exposure to UV rays is higher at altitude. Some days may seem cool in Quito but as it is 9,300 feet (2,850 m) above sea level the sun can be fierce at midday. Wear sunscreen with a high protection factor and reapply regularly. You should also drink plenty of liquids and wear a hat when out during the day to avoid sunstroke, especially on boat trips, where the sun is reflected off the water.

As previously mentioned, locals in Ecuador's main towns and cities drink the tap water, but visitors may want to stick to bottled or filtered water and should also avoid buying raw foods such as salads from street vendors. Ecuadorians swear by *té de orégano* (oregano tea) for an upset stomach, which is very soothing. You will find it at most hotels and guesthouses if you ask.

Yellow fever is only recommended for travelers to some jungle camps on the Amazonian tributaries of Oriente. A yellow fever certificate may be requested at the border if you are entering by land from Peru, so bring it with you.

Malaria is confined to Ecuador's Amazonian jungles, and anti-malarial tablets are recommended for those visiting remote lodges and camps, although seek advice before you go. Other insect-borne diseases include dengue, a flu-like virus spread by day-biting *Aedes aegypti* mosquitoes. Known as breakbone fever (due to the pain felt in joints in extreme cases), there is no vaccination against dengue, so it is important to minimize bites by applying a DEET-based repellant, wearing long sleeves and long pants after sunset, and sleeping under mosquito nets.

Healthcare

There is a two-tier health system in Ecuador: a public health service that is free to all, funded by social security payments (under the Ecuador Social Security system or IESS), and a private system. Big cities, like Quito, Guayaquil, and Cuenca offer excellent healthcare, with modern hospitals and clinics and well-qualified doctors, including specialists who have studied abroad in the US. Despite major investment in the public health system since 2008, when universal healthcare was signed into law, hospitals and clinics in remote areas can still be lacking by Western standards, and there can be long waiting times for surgery or appointments with specialists. The private healthcare sector offers sophisticated scans and lab tests, emergency facilities, plastic surgery, and all major operations for those who can afford to pay.

Expatriates who intend to stay for a long time living or working in Ecuador should take out private health insurance, either through their employer or on their own. Health insurance is mandatory for foreign nationals seeking residency.

For minor ailments, many Ecuadorians first head to the local *farmacía* (drugstore) to ask the pharmacist for advice. Medicines and antibiotics that would need a prescription in the US or northern Europe are often available over the counter. Pharmacists can also give injections. If it's late and your local drugstore is closed it will display a list of the closest pharmacies that are open. You can tell if a drugstore is open by an illuminated sign on the front of the drugstore saying "*Turno.*"

EMERGENCY NUMBERS

Local Emergency: 911	
National Police: 101	
Fire Department: 102	
Red Cross: 131	

NATURAL HAZARDS

Ecuador is a land of high mountains and raging rivers and in the rainy season, especially in unpredictable El Niño years, landslides and flooding are very real dangers. It is also one of the most volcanically active countries in South America with over thirty volcanoes, twenty-three of them active. Volcanoes can also affect major towns and cities. Tungurahua volcano erupted in 2014, spewing ash as high as 33,000 feet (10 km) into the air, forcing residents of the tourist town of Baños to evacuate and officials to divert flights. Tungurahua means "Throat of Fire" in Quechua, and is one of seven active volcanoes that have erupted since the 1930s. In April 2021, Sangay volcano emitted a huge cloud of ash that forced the airport in Guayaquil to close and plunged nearby towns into darkness.

The chance of being caught up in a deadly eruption is slim, given today's sophisticated monitoring equipment and well-practiced evacuation measures, but hikers and climbers should always seek up-to-date advice setting out. In Baños, residents are alerted to the risk of a major blast by sirens. If you hear them while you are there, follow the yellow lines on the streets. They lead to evacuation shelters on the road to Puyo.

Tungurahua volcano, the "Throat of Fire," in central Ecuador, is one of the country's most active volcanoes.

SAFETY

Crime levels in Ecuador are relatively low compared to neighboring Colombia and Peru, but you should always exercise caution, especially in the first few days of your visit. Be particularly careful with your belongings when traveling by bus or taxi, when arriving at new destinations, and in crowded places like markets or festivals. Never carry anything you can't afford to lose or can't claim back on your travel insurance. At night it is always advisable to take taxis and if you can get somebody from your hotel to call one for you from a taxi stand, rather than flagging one down on the street, even better.

There has been a rise in recent years of so-called "express kidnappings" (*secuestro express*), in which victims are held up at gunpoint or with a knife, robbed of their valuables, and taken to ATMs and forced to empty their accounts over a short period of time before being released. Avoid being a target by traveling in a group, and taking money out of ATMs inside a bank and during the day. If you do become involved in an express kidnapping, it is best to give your assailants what they want without a fight.

The main threats to tourists are petty crimes like pickpocketing or bag or camera snatching, so take sensible precautions (see the safety tips below). This is especially true in the historic heart of Quito, the busy hotel, restaurant, and bar area of La Mariscal, and the area around El Panecillo. If taking city buses or the *trole* (tram), be aware that they get very crowded and provide the perfect environment for pickpockets and bag snatchers.

Carry only essentials, have a pouch or money belt under your clothes, split money into different pockets, and wear your daypack on your chest.

Guayaquil has a reputation as the mugging capital of Ecuador, and the area around the docks is particularly unsafe, but tourist areas are fine to visit during the day.

Hot Spots to Avoid

The border with Colombia in the provinces of Carchi, Sucumbios, and northern Esmeraldas is a place to avoid—unless you are using the main border crossing at Tulcán—due to the activities of violent criminal gangs involved in trafficking people and drugs across the border.

TIPS ON STAYING SAFE

- Keep cameras, cell phones, watches, and wallets out of sight, and leave invaluable objects at home.
- Don't use ATMs in the street or at night. Use the ones inside banks during the day.
- Travel with others where possible.
- Learn some Spanish. The more you can speak and understand, the better.
- Listen to the locals. Heed advice on places to avoid.
- Know where you are going. Don't wander around with a map looking lost.
- At night, stick to taxis. Get the number of a reliable company or use a ride-hailing app like EasyTaxi, whose drivers are registered.
- Be wary of pickpockets among crowds and exercise caution when traveling on the buses or trams.
- Use the hotel safe. Don't walk around with all your cash, but have something to hand in case you are mugged.
- Let it go. If you are held up by an armed assailant keep calm and don't resist.
- Have a backup. Keep some bills hidden in your belt or shoes in case of emergency.
- Carry a "mugger's wallet"—a decoy wallet with a few small bills, expired credit card, and a few old library or gym cards for authenticity.
- Scan and e-mail yourself copies of important documents and credit card details in case of theft or loss.

CHAPTER EIGHT

BUSINESS BRIEFING

BUSINESS CULTURE

As elsewhere in South America, who you know is as important as what you have to sell in Ecuador, and networking and building trust is essential. Ecuadorians prefer to do business in person rather than by email or by phone, so face-to-face contact will be crucial to the success of any business venture. The first step is to find people who can set up a meeting for you with decision makers or other important people in an organization, or get things moving if they stall. To make sure you meet the right kind of people, start by consulting the business attaché in your country's embassy or consulate or make contact with local chambers of commerce. Unless they come thoroughly recommended, steer clear of the many *tramitadores* (professional local fixers) offering to cut through red tape, minimize the hold-ups for imports and exports, or set up bank accounts. Depending on the kind of business you plan to do in Ecuador, you'll need legal advice from a recognized local expert to produce and translate contracts.

Status and Hierarchy

Hierarchies are important in Ecuador, especially in the highlands, where formality and the use of titles is fairly widespread. In Ecuador it pays to know some of the usual terms employed when acknowledging the hierarchy of individuals in a company. These give insight into the pecking order in a company, and knowing them will certainly help if you are thinking of relocating, setting up a business, and employing Ecuadorians. It is typical for an engineer to be addressed as *Ingeniero* and a university graduate as *Licenciado* in the same way as a US employee would address a superior as "Sir." Foreign businesspeople are not expected to use these titles, but should be aware of them, and should use *usted* (the formal singular form of "you") when speaking Spanish to senior executives.

DOING BUSINESS WITH ECUADORIANS

Personal Relationships

Generally, Ecuadorians are risk-averse and like to operate in an environment where they know the person they are dealing with, especially in Quito, where old-school formalities are very much the order of the day. This is where the concept of *buena gente* (good people) comes in. If a potential business partner or customer believes you are a good person to do business with, then you have a better chance of sealing a deal. Foreign businesspeople eager to get things moving in Ecuador are often frustrated when initial meetings seem to revolve around social pleasantries—questions about your family and first impressions of Ecuador—rather than getting straight down to business. This is normal. Once a good relationship has been established things will start to move, but not as fast, perhaps, as in the US or the UK. You will also need to put in the time, perhaps over multiple visits, before you see results and make the right contacts.

Dress Code

The dress code in Ecuador is quite formal at meetings and business-related social events. Men typically wear a business suit and tie, although Guayaquil is less formal than Cuenca and Quito. Women should also opt for formal attire, either a skirt or trousers with blouse and jacket, or smart dress. You should also dress formally for a breakfast or lunch meeting, as Ecuadorians will not be impressed if you turn up in jeans and a T-shirt. The same goes for evening events, as companies may invite you to dinner to continue to get to know you. Pack accordingly.

WOMEN IN BUSINESS

Ecuador is still a macho country in many ways, but you are just as likely to be doing business with a woman as with a man in Ecuador. Women are respected as professionals, and businesswomen from abroad will be treated with the same respect. The only difference when meeting a woman in a business environment for the first time is to shake hands when introducing yourself. As for dress, business attire for women is much the same as in the US or the UK.

ARRANGING MEETINGS

When dealing with government bodies the process of making an appointment is formal, bureaucratic, and sometimes very slow. Unless you have a direct contact, it is best to start with contacting your local Ecuadorian embassy by sending a formal letter in Spanish and then following up with an e-mail. If you can get the trade attaché at your embassy in Ecuador to help you with contacts, things will move faster. If you have Ecuadorian agents or partners, even better. With large businesses used to dealing with foreign companies, a direct e-mail in Spanish is acceptable for proposing dates for a meeting but it should be followed up by a phone call the day before to check that everything is on schedule. Entrepreneurs who have spent months sending out e-mails from their home country without any concrete leads will find that once in Ecuador they will start to see progress. This is because Ecuadorians prefer to deal with people face to face, and once they know you personally will be more likely to introduce you to other business acquaintances and help set up meetings. The challenge is to identify who has the power to sign off on deals, and how you can arrange to meet them.

Timing

An important consideration when scheduling appointments is that Ecuadorians take their weekends and public holidays seriously. There is little chance of getting anything done on a Friday afternoon or during the holiday periods like Christmas or Easter. The best time for a meeting is in the morning. Depending on the size of the company, you may be invited to a breakfast meeting with several executives and decision makers where you can discuss things over coffee and a pastry. These often act as pre-meetings and a chance to find out more about you. Don't be frustrated if you don't get down to business straight away. This is not the time to get a decision. The same is true for lunch meetings.

Invitations

An invitation to dinner is probably prompted by the thought of you staying alone in a hotel in an unknown city rather than by a burning desire to do business with you then and there. The etiquette in Ecuador is for the person making the invitation to pay the bill. Never offer to pay half the bill, as it will just look cheap. Offer to pay it all, but don't insist if refused, as this may cause offense. It's better to let your hosts pay, and for you to invite them for the next meal.

Punctuality

The unpredictable nature of traffic and a laid-back attitude to timekeeping by some Ecuadorians can result in a late start when it comes to meetings. Always aim to arrive on time, however, and factor in potential transport delays when making plans. If you do have to wait, even for an hour or so, or end up having to reschedule the meeting for another day, this is nothing personal—it's just a local peculiarity that you will have to get used to. The important thing is not to get ruffled by last-minute changes, and to make sure you leave room in your schedule for such contingencies. Flexibility is key.

MEETINGS AND PRESENTATIONS

The formalities of a meeting usually begin with a greeting to the group of "*Buenos días*" ("Good morning") or "*Buenas tardes*" ("Good afternoon/evening"). Then you will be presented to each person in the room. It is typical to shake hands and use the expression "*Mucho gusto*" ("A pleasure") or "*Es un placer conocerle*" ("It's a pleasure to meet you"). Any materials you bring along should also be translated into Spanish, preferably by a local translator to get the tone right and to avoid words with different meanings in different Spanish-speaking countries.

If you don't speak Spanish, you will need an interpreter or an intermediary or partner who can translate. Generally, senior executives in large private companies will speak English, but there is no guarantee, and junior executives with key expertise pertaining to any deal may have no English at all. When dealing with government agencies you should always bring a translator and have a document drawn up in Spanish with the main points of your proposal. Presentations should also be given in Spanish. Don't be put off if there is conversation during your presentation, or if people take phone calls or leave the room while you are speaking; this is just another example of a more relaxed attitude to doing business.

NEGOTIATIONS

Having given your pitch and answered questions, don't expect an immediate answer. Several meetings will usually be needed before a deal is finalized. You will often be told that somebody else has to be consulted. When dealing with government agencies that is probably the case, but in private firms this could also be a polite way of saying "We'll think about it and get back to you."

If negotiations drag on too long, however, it probably means that the Ecuadorian business is avoiding saying a straight "no" in favor of subtle hints. Having local contacts who are used to the subtleties of Ecuadorian negotiations will help interpret the responses you receive.

CONTRACTS AND LEGAL CONSIDERATIONS

Under the national constitution the government has the right to own certain industries that are considered "strategic," including those related to the oil and gas industry and the generation and distribution of electricity. Contact your embassy or business chamber for the latest updates on the legal status of foreign firms in Ecuador and seek guidance from a well-respected law firm on all the legal issues pertaining to any potential business venture before going ahead.

MANAGING DISAGREEMENT

If there is a disagreement over a contract or payment, the best option is to try to deal with it straight away. Good local legal advice is essential, as going to court over a contract breach can be a protracted and frustrating process. The Ecuadorian legal system is slow, and judicial rulings can be unpredictable. The best way to avoid disputes is to maintain frequent contact with Ecuadorian business partners, which will help to build strong personal ties and flag issues before disputes arise. This may mean a closer working relationship than one would foster with a business partner in the US or UK, and more time spent on the ground.

DEALING WITH RED TAPE

A trip to the bank to make a simple transaction can take some time if it involves foreign transfers, and visits to government offices can involve time-consuming and frustrating phone and e-mail communication, or hours waiting in line. One way to speed things up is to work with local partners, business associations, or reputable agencies that already have contacts and can cut down the time it takes to negotiate the necessary red tape. For importing or exporting goods through customs, a reputable local contact is essential, and local agents are a requirement for dealing with the government.

CORRUPTION

The government has taken steps to stamp out corruption by making it possible to apply for permits and pay taxes online rather than in a crowded public office where a *tramitador* (agent) would charge to speed up the process by greasing palms. However, Ecuador still scores badly overall on Transparency International's Global Corruption Perceptions Index, coming 92 out of 177 countries in 2020, below Chile (21) and Uruguay (27), but above Peru (94). Foreigners doing business in Ecuador should steer clear of any individual or company that offers a shortcut to official procedures through any form of inducement.

GIFT GIVING

Ecuadorian businesses will generally send out small gifts to clients at Christmas. For large firms and multinationals this may include a branded item with the company logo, and for small firms it may be a sample of their product. When first meeting business acquaintances you are not expected to bring gifts, but something typical from your country can act as a good icebreaker. Taxes on imported spirits mean that high-end whiskey brands are something of a treat, so a bottle of Black Label or Chivas Regal will generally be met with appreciation. It may seem obvious, but avoid giving extravagant gifts, especially when bidding for contracts with government agencies, as this can give the wrong impression. Once you get to know your business contacts you can make your choice of gifts more personal.

CHAPTER NINE

COMMUNICATING

LANGUAGE

The official language of Ecuador is Spanish, and well over 95 percent of the population speak it as their first language. There are also some twelve indigenous languages, spoken mainly in the Sierra, the Amazon region of Oriente, and the coastal lowlands, and the vast majority of the people who speak these languages are also fluent in Spanish. A linguistic legacy of the Inca Empire is the prevalence of Quechua, the language of the Inca heartland in Peru that was imposed on the people conquered by the Incas and used as a lingua franca to aid communication. There are nine varieties or dialects of Quechua spoken in Ecuador, but the linguistic differences between a highland Quichua speaker from Otavalo and a Kichwa speaker from the rainforest of the Ecuadorian Amazon are small enough for them to understand each other. One of the distinctive features of the Spanish spoken in Quito and the Sierra is the use of many words borrowed from Quechua.

Ecuadorian Spanish

Ecuadorians will sometimes say that they speak *castellano* (Castilian Spanish), but that doesn't mean they sound like the inhabitants of central Spain and the old Kingdom of Castile. The term harkens back to the days of Columbus and the arrival of the conquistadors, who came from a collection of kingdoms and principalities and independent territories that were not fully unified under the national banner of Spain until the eighteenth century. Variations in the Spanish spoken in Ecuador are linked to the evolution of the language over centuries of distance from Spain and interaction with the speakers of indigenous languages, such as Quechua.

Ecuadorians, especially in Quito, speak quite slowly and clearly, with a pronunciation that is easy to understand if you have some basic Spanish. One difference from the Spanish spoken in Spain that you hear immediately in Ecuador is that it sounds much softer. Also, there is no use of the lisped "c" and "z" that in Spain makes *cerveza* (beer) sound like "thervetha."

People are known for their politeness in the Sierra and speak quite slowly and clearly, with a pronunciation that is easy to understand if you have some basic Spanish. There is a slightly deferential tone to the language in cities like Quito and Cuenca, which is reflected in the use of the formal pronoun *usted* ("you," singular) rather than the informal *tú* when speaking to elders, superiors at work, authority figures, and anybody you are meeting for the first time. It is usual to stick to *usted* until a closer bond has been established, as it shows respect and good manners. Foreigners learning Spanish should follow the cues of the person they are speaking to. If they switch to *tú*, you should follow suit as it indicates a closer, friendlier relationship, and one of equals.

Ecuadorians never use the informal plural *vosotros* ("you") which is used in some Latin American countries. Instead, like Spain, they use *ustedes* for both the formal and informal second-person plural.

Politeness is also evident in the use of diminutives, when *-ito* or *-ita* are added to the end of a noun to make it sound nicer, and more polite. You might hear a taxi driver, for example, insist that there's no need to use his *taxímetro* (meter) because the journey will cost "*Unos dolarcitos, no más!*" ("just a few dollars!").

NO MORE CONFUSION

First-time visitors to Ecuador are sometimes confused by the use of the expression "*no más*" (literally, "no more," or "that's all") which Ecuadorians seem to use after every sentence, especially with instructions or suggestions. "*Sigue, no más*" is a typical way of inviting you to move down the bus and basically means "just keep going." Thus, the popular Ecuadorian song "*Baile, no más!*" translates as "Just Dance," or "Keep Dancing," rather than being an exhortation to stop.

SPEAK LIKE AN ECUADORIAN

There are a number of words and expressions that you will regularly hear in informal conversations in Ecuador. Here's what they mean:

Bacán	Great, excellent, cool
Buenaso	Great, excellent, cool
Cachos	Jokes
Chévere	Great, excellent, cool
Chiro	Broke. *Ando chiro* ("I have no money on me")
Choro	Thief
Chumar	To drink. *Vamos a chumar!* ("Let's have a drink!")
De ley!	For sure! Definitely!
Farra	Party
Mono	Someone from Guayaquil
Vacilar	To flirt

Regional Differences

The people of Quito and the Sierra are known as Serranos, and they can be identified by the use of Quechua words such as *guagua* (baby or child) and *chompa* (light jacket)— see more on Serrano vocabulary and pronunciation below. Serranos have a particular reputation for being respectful and polite in their speech. They show deference to authority figures or superiors at work by using formal verb forms and diminutives, and speak quite softly.

In Guayaquil and on the coast people are louder and livelier, and speak faster. They use fewer expressions from

SPEAK LIKE A SERRANO

Spanish spoken in the Sierra takes many words from Highland Quechua. You won't find these expressions in your English–Spanish dictionary, but knowing what they mean will aid in conversation. The pronunciation is the same as Spanish, so *guagua* sounds like "wa-wa" and *chuta* sounds like "choo-tah." Ñaña is pronounced "nya-nya." Try them out with the people you meet on your travels, and your efforts to speak like a Serrano will likely be greeted with a friendly smile.

Achachai	It's cold, freezing. (For really freezing, you can expand it to *achachachai*.)
Ararai	It's hot, burning
Atatay	Disgusting, horrible
Me cachas?	You get me? Do you understand?
Te cacho	I understand
Chuchaki	Hangover
Chuta!	Wow! (Expression of surprise)
Guagua	Child, baby
Guambra	Young man
Mashi	Friend
Ñaño/Ñaña	Brother/Sister. *Hola ñaño* ("Hi, bro.")
Shunsho	Foolish. *Ese man es medio shunsho* ("That guy is pretty stupid!")

Quechua and more local words, such as *bacán* (amazing) and *chiro* (to be out of cash). One thing you notice among male speakers is the use of a heavily aspirated "*s*" on some words, so that "whiskey" sounds like "wih-ky" and "*no más*" (see above) sounds like "*no mah.*"

Spanglish

With the proliferation of English-language rock and pop songs on the radio, and US TV shows on streaming channels like Netflix, it's not surprising that English words have slipped into the vocabulary of many young Ecuadorians. The usual Spanish word for parking a car is *estacionar*, but you often hear *parquear*. An Ecuadorian might say "*Me voy al mall para hacer shopping*" ("I'm going shopping in the mall"), or "*Necesito un job*" ("I need a job"). The popularity of social media has also led to expressions such as "*Dame un like*" ("Give me a like") and even "*El O El*" ("LOL"). Another unusual crossover is the word *man*, which is used in its English sense except that it can also refer to women and has an unusual plural, *manes.* The result can be sentences like "*Esos dos manes no saben nada de futbol*" ("Those two guys know nothing about soccer").

Speaking Spanish

Ecuadorian children learn some English at school, but outside of hotels and resorts in areas popular with foreign tourists, few people can say much more than a basic "How are you?" or "What is your name?" So, the more Spanish you can pick up before you go the better and once in Ecuador, any attempt to speak Spanish will be met with appreciation, especially if you can use a few basic Ecuadorian expressions. Not only will you be able to ask for things and understand the replies, but you will also find it easier to make meaningful contact with the people you meet. Using a few phrases like "*Sabroso, gracias!*" ("Tasty, thanks"), to show your appreciation of food at dinner, or "*Chévere,*" meaning "cool" or "awesome," when asked what you think of Ecuador, will endear you to your hosts.

Those planning to stay longer in the country can find good schools teaching Spanish to foreigners in Quito, Guayaquil, Cuenca, and beach resorts like Montañita, where you can take classes in between surf sessions. Many schools can arrange home stays with an Ecuadorian family where you get a total immersion in the language and culture. For those with no Spanish, the Duolingo app offers a great way to pick up useful words and phrases, and you may find the Google Translate app very helpful indeed.

Other Languages

Of the twelve indigenous languages spoken in Ecuador, the language group with the most speakers is Quechua, brought to Ecuador by the Incas. Ecuadorian Quechua belongs to the Northern Quechua group, a branch of the Quechuan language. Spoken by approximately 10 million indigenous people from southern Colombia to northern Argentina, it is the most widely spoken indigenous language in the Americas.

Other indigenous languages include Cofán, Siona, Tetete, Secoya, Waorani, Shuar, Achuar–Shiwiar, and Záparo in the Amazonian region of Oriente; and Cha'palaachi (Cayapa), Colorado, and Awa–Cuaiquer in the Western coastal lowlands. All Ecuador's indigenous languages are classified as endangered, as there is no formal teaching of them in schools and labor migration has broken up traditional indigenous communities, leading to the adoption of Spanish as a main language.

FACE TO FACE

Having good manners and showing respect for others is very important in Ecuador. When entering a shop or office people will normally say to those present "*Buenos días*" ("good day") or "*buenas tardes*" ("good afternoon").

Elderly people are treated with respect and addressed as *Señor/Señora* or even more respectfully as *Don/Doña*. *Señorita* is the equivalent of "Miss" in English (there's no equivalent of Ms.).

When being introduced it is customary to say "*mucho gusto*" ("pleased to meet you") or "*un placer*" ("it's a pleasure"), followed by your first name.

When meeting, men will shake hands or go for the full bear hug and backslap. The etiquette between women, or a man and a woman who know each other, is a single kiss on the right cheek. An air kiss is sufficient. Greetings might start with a simple: *Hola, que tal?* ("Hi, how are you?").

In restaurants or at dinner it is customary to say "*Buen provecho*" ("Enjoy your meal") to other diners. When dining at home with an Ecuadorian family the meal may start with somebody saying grace, and it is customary to bow your head while they give thanks to God for the food on the table.

BODY LANGUAGE

Nonverbal communication doesn't play as big a part in the lives of Ecuadorians as it does in, say, Cuba, Venezuela, or Argentina, where people talk with their hands and gestures can seem quite dramatic. In the Sierra people are more reserved with their body language, but even there they don't have the same limits on personal space as people in the US or Europe, and you will find that people are tactile and will hug and touch their friends and acquaintances which demonstrates closeness.

When it comes to gestures, there are only a few to bear in mind. In Ecuador, it is considered rude to point a finger at somebody. Instead, to point, people pucker their lips in the direction of the person or thing they want to point at. They will also beckon someone over with the palm down rather than up.

When at a restaurant, let the waiter know you would like the bill by catching their eye and scribbling with your finger on the palm of your hand.

HUMOR

Ecuadorians like to laugh, and their humor can be quite earthy, considering the reputation they have among other Spanish-speaking countries for being polite and reserved. They also like to share a joke (*un cacho*) or two when in company. Most jokes are quite innocent, based on a play of words, though you may also hear jokes about women or homosexuals that will sound rather outdated to visitors from the US or Europe.

Comedy staples include good-looking girls in tight outfits parading around for the benefit of older men, domineering mothers-in-law, and wives with rolling pins waiting for a worse-for-wear husband who comes home with lipstick on his collar. A popular character in comedies is a man whose wife controls him, known as a *mandarina*—a clever use of the verb *mandar* (to order) and the word for a mandarin orange.

Strong regional rivalries mean that Serranos and Costeños make jokes about each other that are far from polite, while the people of Tulcán, known as Pastuzos, are singled out for jokes that question their intelligence.

My Mother-in-Law

"Yesterday, two guys in the street shouted abuse at my mother-in-law."

"Did you intervene?"

"No, three people shouting abuse at her would have been too much."

THE MEDIA

The Ecuadorian media landscape changed considerably in 2017 when former President Moreno came to power. Before that, his predecessor President Correa had waged a ten year war on the media during his two terms in office, which saw tighter regulations placed on the media, government takeovers of media outlets, and legal action pursued by the president against newspapers and individual journalists.

Correa argued that the private media in Ecuador was run by powerful economic and political interest groups who for too long were able to print what they liked and that they should face legal consequences if they publish defamatory, inflammatory, or erroneous reports aimed at undermining his government.

Correa's aggressive attitude to the press at home was labeled hypocritical when in 2012 WikiLeaks founder Julian Assange was offered political asylum after he sought sanctuary in the Ecuadorian Embassy in London.

Criticism of Correa's attacks on the media only increased after a new Communications Law was passed in 2013. The law created a new regulating body with the power to impose fines on media outlets, and new restrictions against what it called *linchamiento mediatico*, or media lynching. Restrictions were also placed on publishing or broadcasting material that could incite violence or racial or religious hatred.

The measures resulted in increased self-censorship by private media, with one editor of Ecuador's most popular daily papers, *Hoy*, saying that the media faced "a field full of land mines where no one can work with freedom and confidence." The Correa government insisted that the new law restored "balance" in the media but critics called it a *ley mordaza* (gag law).

Once in power, Moreno took a much more media-friendly approach, reaching out to private media groups and encouraging investigative journalism. In 2018, the National Assembly eliminated the controversial body created under the 2013 Communication Law and in 2021 incoming President Guillermo Lasso put forward a new Freedom of Expression and Communication Law that would do away with the limits on press freedom imposed under Correa.

MAIL

The national postal system, Correos del Ecuador, has offices in all major cities and towns and a distribution system covering the whole country and transfer abroad. Post offices are open from Mondays to Saturdays from 7:30 a.m. to 7:30 p.m. There are no registered, certified, or priority mail options, and delivery can be slow, taking anything from a week or two to send or receive letters and parcels from the US and longer for mail to Europe. More reliable are international courier companies, such as FedEx and DHL, which have offices in Ecuador's main cities. Whoever you use to receive parcels, be aware that the tax payable on imported goods is high and goods will not be released until it is paid.

CELL PHONES AND SIM CARDS

Some areas of Ecuador have no landline service due to the difficulty and the cost of laying copper cable connections to remote and high-altitude locations.

Ecuadorians have a choice of cell phone contracts offering calls, messages and data, but visitors can buy a SIM card with a pay-as-you-go option. SIM-only options start from around $20 a month and can be set up in Quito airport as well as cell phone stores and kiosks around the country. Pay-as-you-go customers can add credit by buying top-up cards, or electronically at newspaper kiosks, supermarkets, cell-repair stores, and stores where the sign *recargas* ("top up") is displayed. The two biggest mobile providers are Claro and Movistar—Claro has a slight edge in terms of national coverage. Both offer pay-as-you-go options and pre-paid packages for visitors.

Some Ecuadorians carry two or even three cell phones for juggling business and private calls and getting the best deals on the different networks.

INTERNET AND SOCIAL MEDIA

Ecuador has a growing number of Internet users and in 2021 around 57 percent of the population were regular users. Given the extreme nature of the country's geography, Internet coverage is good, with fast and reliable broadband in the main towns and cities. Most hotels, restaurants, and upmarket cafés offer free Wi-Fi, especially in the main cities of Quito, Guayaquil, and Cuenca, and popular tourist spots like Baños, Montañita, and the Galápagos Islands. In Quito, for example, the local authorities provide free Wi-Fi service in the city's many parks and plazas and at the bus station at Quitumbe. In remote jungle areas and mountain towns, where coverage can be sketchy, you can generally find a cybercafé offering a connection for anything from 50 cents to $1.50 an hour, though these are slowly becoming a thing of the past as coverage improves and smartphone ownership increases.

As you will have picked up by now, Ecuadorians are extremely sociable and love to spend time together, so it is no surprise that social networking sites are popular here too. In 2021 there were some 14 million social media users, an impressive 17 percent increase on the previous year, the coronavirus pandemic and associated lockdowns no doubt playing a part. The top social media apps in Ecuador are Facebook, Twitter, Instagram, and TikTok while WhatsApp is the most used messaging service. (See page 198 for more on cell phone apps worth having.) To make calls without a cell phone, head for the nearest cybercafé or *locutorio* (communications center). These stores usually have a few computers with headsets and webcams so you can use Skype and phone booths where you can make calls abroad.

CONCLUSION

First-time visitors to this small South American country are quickly won over by the warmth of its people and amazed by its incredible biodiversity, world-class bird watching, and historic cities.

Dramatic snow-capped volcanoes in the Andes, dense rainforests in the Amazon, and unique island habitats off the coast are all packed into such a small space it is possible to experience the best Ecuador has to offer in one carefully planned visit and still leave enough for further exploration.

Ecuador has evolved from a major exporter of bananas to an oil nation that must grapple with the environmental consequences of exploiting this important source of state revenue while respecting the rights of the rainforest tribes whose jungle homes lie on top of huge oil reserves. Home to the first two UNESCO World Heritage Sites, the city of Quito and the Galapagos Islands, Ecuador has an enormous tourism potential that could—if managed carefully—offer a sustainable alternative to oil.

The enforced slump as a result of coronavirus restrictions exacerbated wider economic difficulty brought about by mismanagement under the Moreno government, but tourism has begun to pick up pace again, and new political leaders offer a possible return to the positive economic trajectory achieved under Correa.

Armed with the careful research outlined in this overview, we hope that tourists, business travelers, and those wishing to relocate to Ecuador will now have the confidence to delve more deeply into this fascinating country and engage more purposefully with its rich artistic and gastronomic traditions, linguistic quirks, and indigenous cultures.

FURTHER READING

Arana, Marie. *Bolivar: American Liberator*. New York: Simon & Schuster, 2014

Grigsby Crawford. J. *The Gringo. A Memoir*. Washington: Wild Elephant Press, 2012.

Halls, Monty. *My Family and the Galápagos*. London: Headline, 2021.

Hemming, John. *The Conquest of the Incas*. Boston: Mariner Books, 2003.

Horwell, David, Oxford, Peter. *Galápagos Wildlife*. Chesham: Bradt, 2020.

Icaza, Jorge. *Huasipungo (The Villagers)*. Carbondale: Southern Illinois University Press, 1964.

Jacobs, Michael. *Andes*. London: Granta, 2011.

MacQuarrie, Kim. *The Last Days of the Incas*. New York: Simon & Schuster, 2008.

Miller, Tom. *The Panama Hat Trail*. New York: National Geographic, 2001.

Murray, Pamela S. *For Glory and Bolívar*: The Remarkable Life of Manuela Sáenz. Texas University Press, 2010.

Restall, Robin, Freile, Juan. *Birds of Ecuador*. London: Helm Field Guides, 2018.

Striffler, Steve, de la Torre, Carlos. *The Ecuador Reader: History, Culture, Politics*. Durham: Duke University Press Books, 2009.

Vonnegut, Kurt. *Galápagos: A Novel*. New York: Dial Press, 2009.

Whitaker, Robert. *The Mapmaker's Wife: A True Tale of Love, Murder, and Survival in the Amazon*. London: Delta, 2004.

USEFUL APPS

Ecuadorians, just like the rest of the world, are increasingly turning to smartphone apps when it comes to communicating, shopping, or looking for love. Here are some apps you may find helpful:

COMMUNICATION

Whatsapp The most popular messaging app in Ecuador, and the preferred form of communication with hotels, restaurants, drivers, tour guides and business contacts.

Facebook, **Instagram**, and **TikTok** The most widely used social media apps in Ecuador.

Google Translate Many a traveler's go-to translation app, with audio playback of phrases and direct text translation for menus and signs.

TRANSPORTATION

Moovit For timetables and booking public transport.

EasyTaxi For booking a cab in Quito, Cuenca, or Guayaquil.

Uber currently operates in Ambato, Guayaquil, Ibarra, Machala, Manta, Quito, Salinas, and Santo Domingo de Los Colorados.

WAZE The most popular local GPS navigation app.

Tripadvisor A mine of information on hotels, restaurants, and tours, with user reviews.

SHOPPING

Glovo and **UberEats** For food home delivery.

Rappi For delivery of groceries and restaurant orders.

Tipti for ordering and delivering groceries and household items.

PICTURE CREDITS

INDEX

Acknowledgments

This book would not have been possible without the help and advice of many people in Ecuador. First and foremost are my good friends Digna Martinez in Quito, and Nadia de la Gasca in Guayaquil who gave me invaluable insights into Ecuadorian daily life. I must also thank Dominic Hamilton of Metropolitan Touring and editor of the fabulous *Ñan* magazine. This book is dedicated to my son Francisco and my amazing mum, Shirley.